Clusters for High Availability

A Primer of HP Solutions

Second Edition

ISBN 0-13-089355-2

9 780130 893550

90000

Hewlett-Packard® Professional Books

OPERATING SYSTEMS

Fernandez	Configuring CDE: The Common Desktop Environment
Lund	Integrating UNIX and PC Network Operating Systems
Madell	Disk and File Management Tasks on HP-UX
Poniatowski	HP-UX 11i System Administration Handbook and Toolkit
Poniatowski	HP-UX 11.x System Administration Handbook and Toolkit
Poniatowski	HP-UX 11.x System Administration "How To" Book
Poniatowski	HP-UX System Administration Handbook and Toolkit
Poniatowski	Learning the HP-UX Operating System
Poniatowski	UNIX User's Handbook
Rehman	HP Certified, HP-UX System Administration
Roberts	UNIX and Windows 2000 Interoperability Guide
Sauers, Weygant	HP-UX Tuning and Performance
Stone, Symons	UNIX Fault Management
Weygant	Clusters for High Availability: A Primer of HP Solutions, Second Edition

ONLINE/INTERNET

Amor	The E-business (R)evolution: Living and Working in an Interconnected Wo
Greenberg, Lakeland	A Methodology for Developing and Deploying Internet and Intranet Soluti
Greenberg, Lakeland	Building Professional Web Sites with the Right Tools
Klein	Building Enhanced HTML Help with DHTML and CSS
Werry, Mowbray	Online Communities: Commerce, Community Action, and the Virtual University

NETWORKING/COMMUNICATIONS

Blommers	OpenView Network Node Manager: Designing and Implementing an Enterprise Solution
Blommers	Practical Planning for Network Growth
Bruce, Dempsey	Security in Distributed Computing: Did You Lock the Door?
Lucke	Designing and Implementing Computer Workgroups

ENTERPRISE

Blommers	Architecting Enterprise Solutions with UNIX Networking
Cook	Building Enterprise Information Architectures
Missbach/Hoffmann	SAP Hardware Solutions: Servers, Storage, and Networks for mySAP.com
Pipkin	Halting the Hacker: A Practical Guide to Computer Security
Pipkin	Information Security: Protecting the Global Enterprise
Thornburgh	Fibre Channel for Mass Storage
Thornburgh, Schoenborn	Storage Area Networks: Designing and Implementing a Mass Storage Syste
Todman	Designing a Data Warehouse: Supporting Customer Relationship Management

Clusters for High Availability

A Primer of HP Solutions

Second Edition

Peter S. Weygant
Hewlett-Packard Company

www.hp.com/hpbooks

Prentice Hall PTR
Upper Saddle River, New Jersey 07458
www.phptr.com

Library of Congress Cataloging-in-Publication Data

Weygant, Peter.
    Clusters for high availability : a primer of HP solutions / Peter S. Weygant.--2nd ed.
        p. cm.
    ISBN 0-13-089355-2
            1. Hewlett-Packard computers.   2. Systems availability.   I. Title.
        QA76.8.H48 W49 2001
        004'.36--dc21   2001021151

Editorial/Production Supervision: *Donna Cullen-Dolce*
Acquisitions Editor: *Jill Harry*
Editorial Assistant: *Justin Somma*
Marketing Manager: *Dan DePasquale*
Manufacturing Buyer: *Maura Zaldivar*
Cover Design: *Talar Agasyan*
Cover Design Director: *Jerry Votta*
Manager, Hewlett-Packard Retail Book Publishing: *Patricia Pekary*
Editor, Hewlett-Packard Professional Books: *Susan Wright*

ISBN 0-13-089355-2

HP Part Number B3936-90047

Prentice-Hall International (UK) Limited, London
Prentice-Hall of Australia Pty. Limited, Sydney
Prentice-Hall Canada Inc., Toronto
Prentice-Hall Hispanoamericana, S.A., Mexico
Prentice-Hall of India Private Limited, New Delhi
Prentice-Hall of Japan, Inc., Tokyo
Pearson Education Asia Pte. Ltd.
Editora Prentice-Hall do Brasil, Ltda., Rio de Janeiro
Prentice-Hall, Inc., Upper Saddle River, New Jersey

Dedicated to the engineers in the
Availability Clusters Solutions Laboratory
at Hewlett-Packard

Contents

Contents

Contents

Contents

Contents

Contents

Contents

Contents

Contents

Contents

Contents

List of Figures

List of Figures

List of Figures

List of Figures

Foreword

The author and I have had the good fortune to work in HP's high availability lab for over six years now. In this time, we have spoken with many, many customers who have expressed a need to understand how to enable their businesses to operate in a world that demands ever-increasing levels of uptime. The explosive development of the Internet and the resulting emphasis on e-business, e-commerce, and e-services has made high availability a requirement for an ever-growing range of systems.

At the same time, Hewlett-Packard's cluster software products—MC/ServiceGuard and ServiceGuard OPS Edition (formerly known as MC/LockManager)—have grown in functionality, and the range of supported hardware devices—disks, disk arrays, networks, and system processing units—has also expanded. In addition, more HP-UX system administrators are now confronting the issues of configuring and monitoring high availability systems.

Today, it is still HP's goal to provide a complete range of solutions that yield an **always-on infrastructure** for commercial computing of the 21st century. Peter Weygant's book is intended to assist readers in developing a greater understanding of the concepts, choices, and recommendations for achieving optimal availability in their environments.

Wesley Sawyer
Hewlett-Packard Computing Systems Group
Availability Clusters Solutions Laboratory Manager

Foreword to the 1996 Edition

Over the last ten years, UNIX systems have moved from the specialized role of providing desktop computing power for engineers into the broader arena of commercial computing. This evolution is the result of continual dramatic improvements in functionality, reliability, performance, and supportability. We are now well into the next phase of the UNIX evolution: providing solutions for mission-critical computing.

To best meet the requirements of the data center for availability, scalability, and flexibility, Hewlett-Packard has developed a robust cluster architecture for HP-UX that combines multiple systems into a *high availability cluster*. Individual computers, known as *nodes*, are connected in a loosely-coupled manner, each maintaining its own separate processors, memory, operating system, and storage devices. Special system processes bind these nodes together and allow them to cooperate to provide outstanding levels of availability and flexibility for supporting mission-critical applications. The nodes in a cluster can be configured either to share data on a set of disks or to obtain exclusive access to data.

To maintain Hewlett-Packard's commitment to the principles of open systems, our high availability clusters use standards-based hardware components such as SCSI disks and Ethernet LANs. There are no proprietary APIs that force vendor lock-in, and most applications will run on a high availability cluster without modification.

As the world's leading vendor of open systems, Hewlett-Packard is especially proud to publish this primer on cluster solutions for high availability. Peter Weygant has done a fine job of presenting the basic concepts, architectures, and terminology used in HP's cluster solutions. This is the place to begin your exploration of the world of high availability clusters.

Xuan Bui
Hewlett-Packard General Systems Division
Research and Development Laboratory Manager

Preface

Since the initial publication of this book in 1996, the installed base of Hewlett-Packard's high availability (HA) clusters has grown to more than 45,000 licenses sold worldwide. The technology itself has matured, incorporating such diverse features as event monitoring, wide area networks (WANs), storage area networks (SANs), clusters of up to 16 nodes, and on-line configuration of most cluster components. Hundreds of thousands of users are employing ServiceGuard clusters for tasks as diverse as Internet access, telecommunications billing, manufacturing process control, and banking, to mention only a few.

Hewlett-Packard HA clusters are now or soon will be available on multiple platforms, including HP-UX, Linux, and Windows. Today, HP's *5nines:5minutes* HA continuum provides products, integrated solutions, and reference architectures that allow users to achieve the highest levels of availability—with as little as five minutes of downtime per year. These efforts show a continuing, ongoing commitment to developing tools and products that approach the vision of 99.999% HA.

The three pillars of Hewlett-Packard's HA computing are robust technology, sound computing processes, and proactive customer support. This guide describes these three aspects of HA solutions in the world of enterprise clusters. It presents basic concepts and terms, then describes the use of cluster technology to provide highly available open systems solutions for the commercial enterprise. Here is an overview of each chapter's topics:

Preface

- Chapter 1, "Basic High Availability Concepts," presents the language used to describe highly available systems and components, and introduces ways of measuring availability. It also highlights the processes needed to keep systems available.

- Chapter 2, "Clustering to Eliminate Single Points of Failure," shows how to identify and eliminate single points of failure by implementing a cluster architecture.

- Chapter 3, "High Availability Cluster Components," is an overview of HP's current roster of HA software and hardware offerings.

- Chapter 4, "Cluster Monitoring and Management," describes a selection of tools for monitoring, mapping, and managing HA clusters.

- Chapter 5, "Disaster-Tolerant High Availability Systems," is an introduction to disaster-tolerant cluster architectures, which extend the geographic range of the HA cluster.

- Chapter 6, "Enterprise-Wide High Availability Solutions," describes hardware and software components and processes that provide the highest levels of availability for today's environment of e-business, e-commerce, and e-services, including 5nines:5minutes.

- Chapter 7, "Sample High Availability Solutions," discusses a few concrete examples of highly available cluster solutions.

- Chapter 8, "Glossary of High Availability Terminology," gives definitions of important words and phrases used to describe HA and HP's HA products and solutions.

Additional information is available in the HP publications *Managing MC/ServiceGuard* and *Configuring OPS Clusters with MC/LockManager.* The *HP 9000 Servers Configuration Guide* and the *HP Net Servers Configuration Guide* contain detailed information about supported HA configurations. These and other more specialized documents on enterprise clusters are available from your HP representative.

Acknowledgments

This book has benefited from the careful review of many individuals inside and outside of Hewlett-Packard. The author gratefully acknowledges the contributions of these colleagues, many of whom are listed here: Will Abrams, Joe Bac, Bob Baird, Trent Bass, Dan Beringer, Kyle Black, Claude Brazell, Thomas Buenermann, Xuan Bui, Karl-Heinz Busse, Bruce Campbell, Larry Cargnoni, Sally Carl, Gina Cassinelli, Marian Cochran, Annie Cooperman, Ron Czinski, Dan Dickerman, Larry Dino, Jay Elkerton, Janie Felix, John Foxcroft, Shivaji Ganesh, Janet Gee, Mike Gutter, Terry Hand, Michael Hayward, Frank Ho, Cathy Huang, Margaret Hunter, Lisa Iarkowski, Art Ipri, Michael Kahn, Bethany Kanui, Marty King, Clark Macaulay, Gary Marcos, Debby McIsaac, Doug McKenzie, Tim Metcalf, Parissa Mohamadi, Alex Morgan, Markus Ostrowicki, Bob Ramer, Bob Sauers, David Scott, Dan Shive, Christine Smith, Paul Sneed, Eric Soderberg, Steve Stichler, Tim Stockwell, Brad Stone, Liz Tam, Bob Togasaki, Susan Townsend, Emil Velez, Tad Walsh, and Bev Woods.

Joseph Algieri, Pam Dickerman, and Wesley Sawyer graciously agreed to review the manuscript of the second edition, which has incorporated many of their suggestions.

Thanks to Jill Harry, Acquisitions Editor at Prentice Hall PTR, for her continued support and gentle nudging. Thanks to production editor Donna Cullen-Dolce for her scrupulous attention to detail in preparing the manuscript. And thanks also to Pat Pekary and Susan Wright, editors at HP Professional Books, for their guidance and help.

Acknowledgments

Additional thanks to those groups of Hewlett-Packard customers who read and commented on early versions of the manuscript. And finally, a special thank you to the individuals who pointed out mistakes in the first edition and suggested changes and additions for the second edition. Errors and omissions are the author's sole responsibility.

About the Author

Peter S. Weygant is a Learning Products Engineer in the Availability Clusters Solutions laboratory at Hewlett-Packard. Formerly a professor of English, he has been a technical writer and consultant in the computer industry for the last 20 years. He has developed documentation and managed publication projects in the areas of digital imaging, relational database technology, performance tuning, and high availability systems. He has a BA degree in English Literature from Colby College as well as MA and PhD degrees in English from the University of Pennsylvania. He is the co-author (with Robert F. Sauers) of *HP-UX Tuning and Performance: Concepts, Tools, and Methods*, also published by Prentice Hall PTR in the Hewlett-Packard Professional Books series.

Clusters for High Availability

A Primer of HP Solutions

Second Edition

CHAPTER 1
Basic High Availability Concepts

*T*his book begins by taking an elementary look at high availability (HA) computing and how it is implemented through enterprise-level cluster solutions. We start in this chapter with some of the basic concepts of HA. Here's what we'll cover:

- What Is High Availability?
- High Availability as a Business Requirement
- What Are the Measures of High Availability?
- Understanding the Obstacles to High Availability
- Preparing Your Organization for High Availability
- The Starting Point for a Highly Available System
- Moving to High Availability

Later chapters will explore the implementation of HA in clusters, then describe HP's HA products in more detail. A separate chapter is devoted to concrete examples of business solutions that use HA.

What Is High Availability?

Before exploring the implications of HA in computer systems, we need to define some terms. What do we mean by phrases like "availability," "high availability," and "high availability computing?"

Available

The term **available** describes a system that provides a specific level of service as needed. This idea of availability is part of everyday thinking. In computing, availability is generally understood as the period of time when services are available (for instance, 16 hours a day, six days a week) or as the time required for the system to respond to users (for example, under one-second response time). Any loss of service, whether planned or unplanned, is known as an **outage**. **Downtime** is the duration of an outage measured in units of time (e.g., minutes or hours).

Highly Available

Figure 1.1 *Highly Available Services: Electricity*

Highly available characterizes a system that is designed to avoid the loss of service by reducing or managing failures as well as minimizing planned downtime for the system. We expect a service to be *highly* available when life, health, and well-being, including the economic well-being of a company, depend on it.

For example, we expect electrical service to be highly available (Figure 1.1). All but the smallest, shortest outages are unacceptable, since we have geared our lives to depend on electricity for refrigeration, heating, and lighting, in addition to less important daily needs.

Even the most highly available services occasionally go out, as anyone who has experienced a blackout or brownout in a large city can attest (Figure 1.2). But in these cases, we expect to see an effort to restore service at once. When a failure occurs, we expect the electric company to be on the road fixing the problem as soon as possible.

Figure 1.2 *Service Outage*

Highly Available Computing

In many businesses, the availability of computers has become just as important as the availability of electric power itself. **Highly available computing** uses computer systems which are designed and managed to operate with only a small amount of planned and unplanned downtime.

Note that *highly available* is not absolute. The needs of different businesses for HA are quite diverse. International businesses, companies running multiple shifts, and many Internet sites may require user access to databases around the clock. Financial institutions must be able to transfer funds at any time of night or day, seven days a week. On the other hand, some retail businesses may require the computer to be available only 18 hours a day, but during those 18 hours, they may require sub-second response time for transaction processing.

Service Levels

The **service level** of a system is the degree of service the system will provide to its users. Often, the service level is spelled out in a document known as the service level agreement (SLA). The service levels your business requires determine the kinds of applications you develop, and HA systems provide the hardware and software framework in which these applications can work effectively to provide the needed level of service. High availability implies a service level in which both *planned* and *unplanned* computer outages do not exceed a small stated value.

Continuous Availability

Continuous availability means non-stop service, that is, there are no planned or unplanned outages at all. This is a much more ambitious goal than HA, because there can be no lapse in service. In effect, continuous availability is an ideal state rather than a characteristic of any real-world system.

This term is sometimes used to indicate a very high level of availability in which only a very small known quantity of downtime is acceptable. Note that HA does *not* imply continuous availability.

Fault Tolerance

Fault tolerance is not a degree of availability so much as a method for achieving very high levels of availability. A fault-tolerant system is characterized by redundancy in most hardware components, including CPU, memory, I/O subsystems, and other elements. A fault-tolerant system is one that has the ability to continue service in spite of a hardware or software failure. However, even fault-tolerant systems are subject to outages from human error. Note that HA does *not* imply fault tolerance.

Disaster Tolerance

Disaster tolerance is the ability of a computer installation to withstand multiple outages, or the outage of all the systems at a single site. For HP server installations, disaster tolerance is achieved by locating systems on multiple sites and providing architected solutions that allow one site to take over in the event of a disaster. The multiple sites in a disaster-tolerant system may be distributed across a single campus, they may be located in different buildings in the same metropolitan area, or they may be dispersed as widely as across a continent or on opposite sides of an ocean. Solutions like these offer the greatest amount of protection for mission-critical data. Needless to say, they can be very expensive to implement, and they all require very careful planning and implementation.

5nines:5minutes

In 1998, HP management committed to a new vision for HA in open systems: 99.999% availability, with no more than five minutes of downtime per year. This ambitious goal has driven the development of many specialized hardware and software facilities by a number of vendors working in partnership. As of the year 2001, HP's own contributions include new generations of fault-resilient HP 9000 systems, improvements in the HP-UX operating system, new software solutions, and extensive monitoring tools that make it possible to measure downtime with a high degree of precision. Many of these improvements have been added back into the standard HP hardware and software products in a kind of "trickle-down" of technological improvement.

Not all users need every type of device or tool used to provide availability levels as high as 99.999%. Not all users wish to pay the price that such tools command in the marketplace. But everyone benefits from the effort to meet the goal of a very high degree of availability as the technology advances. Consider the analogy of race car engines: Even though you don't expect to see a race car engine in a family sedan, the technology used in building and improving the race car engine eventually ends up improving the sedan anyway.

E-vailable Computing

The phenomenal expansion of Internet business activity has created the need to define yet another type of availability: **e-vailability**, the availability of a server to support fast access to a Web site. It is well known that at periods of peak demand, Web sites suffer performance degradation to the point that users cancel an attempted transaction in frustration at waiting too long or at being refused access temporarily. E-vailability is a combination of the traditional kinds of availability described earlier in this chapter and sufficient server performance and capacity to meet peak demands. Figure 1.3 shows the relationship of availability, performance, and capacity to achieve high levels of e-vailability.

By managing the components of e-vailability, you can allocate different levels of availability to different users depending on their standing as customers. For example, the premier customer class might be given the quickest access to a Web site, say under one second, whereas ordinary customers might get access in one to five seconds, and non-customers (simple Internet cruisers) might obtain access in five to ten seconds. Thus within the framework of e-vailability, HA can be a commodity that customers pay for, or it can be a reward for loyalty or high spending levels.

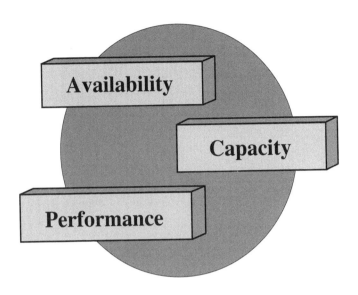

Figure 1.3 *Components of E-vailability*

Matching Availability to User Needs

A failure affects availability when it results in an unplanned loss of service that lasts long enough to create a problem for users of the system. User sensitivity will depend on the specific application. For example, a failure that is corrected within one second may not result in any perceptible loss of service in an environment that does on-line transaction processing (OLTP); but for a scientific application that runs in a real-time environment, one second may be an unacceptable interval.

Since any component can fail, the challenge is to design systems in which problems can be predicted and isolated before a failure occurs and in which failures are quickly detected and corrected when they happen.

Choosing a Solution

Your exact requirement for availability determines the kind of solution you need. For example, if the loss of a system for a few hours of planned downtime is acceptable to you, then you may not need to purchase storage products with hot pluggable disks. On the other hand, if you cannot afford a planned period of maintenance during which a disk replacement can be performed on a mirrored disk system, then you may wish to consider an HA disk array that supports hot plugging or hot swapping of components. (Descriptions of these HA products appear in later sections.)

Keep in mind that some HA solutions are becoming more affordable. The trickle-down effect has resulted in improvements in HP's Intel-based NetServer systems, and there has been considerable growth in the number of clustering solutions available for PCs that use the Windows and Linux operating systems.

High Availability as a Business Requirement

In the current business climate, HA computing is a requirement, not a luxury. From one perspective, HA is a form of insurance against the loss of business due to computer downtime. From another point of view, HA provides new opportunities by allowing your company to provide better and more competitive customer service.

High Availability as Insurance

High availability computing is often seen as insurance against the following kinds of damage:

- Loss of income
- Customer dissatisfaction
- Missed opportunities

For commercial computing, a highly available solution is needed when loss of the system results in loss of revenue. In such cases, the application is said to be *mission-critical*. For all mission-critical applications—that is, where income may be lost through downtime—HA is a requirement. In banking, for example, the ability to obtain certain account balances 24 hours a day may be mission-critical. In parts of the securities business, the need for HA may only be for that portion of the day when a particular stock market is active; at other times, systems may be safely brought down.

High Availability as Opportunity

Highly available computing provides a business opportunity, since there is an increasing demand for "around-the-clock" computerized services in areas as diverse as banking and financial market operations, communications, order entry and catalog services, resource management, and others. It is not possible to give a simple definition of when an application is mission-critical or of when a highly available application creates new opportunities; this depends on the nature of the business. However, in any business that depends on computers, the following principles are always true:

- The degree of availability required is determined by business needs. There is no absolute amount of availability that is right for all businesses.
- There are many ways to achieve HA.
- The means of achieving HA affects all aspects of the system.
- The likelihood of failure can be reduced by creating an infrastructure that stresses clear procedures and preventive maintenance.
- Recovery from failures must be planned.

Some or all of the following are expectations for the software applications that run in mission-critical environments:

- There should be a low rate of application failure, that is, a maximum time between failures.
- Applications should be able to recover after failure.
- There should be minimal scheduled downtime.
- The system should be configurable without shutdown.
- System management tools must be available.

Cost of High Availability

As with other kinds of insurance, the cost depends on the degree of availability you choose. Thus, the value of HA to the enterprise is directly related to the costs of outages. The higher the cost of an outage, the easier it becomes to justify the expense of HA solutions. As the degree of availability approaches the ideal of 100% availability, the cost of the solution increases more rapidly. Thus, the cost of 99.95% availability is significantly greater than the cost of 99.5% availability, the cost of 99.5% availability is significantly greater than 99%, and so on.

What Are the Measures of High Availability?

Availability and reliability can be described in terms of numbers, though doing so can be very misleading. In fact, there is no standard method for modeling or calculating the degree of availability in a computer system. The important thing is to create clear definitions of what the numbers mean and then use them consistently. Remember that availability is not a measurable attribute of a system like CPU clock speed. Availability can only be measured historically, based on the behavior of the actual system. Moreover, in measuring availability, it is important to ask not simply, "Is the application available?" but, "Is the entire system providing service at the proper level?"

Availability is related to reliability, but they are not the same thing. Availability is the percentage of total system time the computer system is accessible for normal usage. Reliability is the amount of time before a system is expected to fail. Availability includes reliability.

Calculating Availability

The formula in Figure 1.4 defines availability as the portion of time that a unit can be used. Elapsed time is continuous time (operating time + downtime).

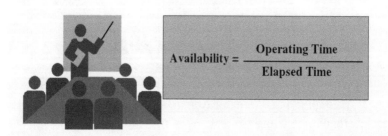

$$Availability = \frac{Operating\ Time}{Elapsed\ Time}$$

Figure 1.4 Availability

Availability is usually expressed as a percentage of hours per week, month, or year during which the system and its services can be used for normal business.

Expected Period of Operation

Measures of availability must be seen against the background of the organization's expected period of operation of the system. The following tables show the actual hours of uptime and downtime associated with different percentages of availability for two common periods of operation.

Table 1.1 shows 24x7x365, which stands for a system that is expected to be in use 24 hours a day, 7 days a week, 365 days a year.

Table 1.1 *Uptime and Downtime for a 24x7x365 System*

Availability	Minimum Expected Hours of Uptime	Maximum Allowable Hours of Downtime	Remaining Hours
99%	8672	88	0
99.5%	8716	44	0
99.95%	8755	5	0
100%	8760	0	0

The table shows that there is no remaining time on the system at all. All the available time in the year (8760 hours) is accounted for. This means that all maintenance must be carried out either when the system is up or during the allowable downtime hours. In addition, the higher the percentage of availability, the less time allowed for failure.

Table 1.2 shows a 12x5x52 system, which is expected to be up for 12 hours a day, 5 days a week, 52 weeks a year. In such an example, the normal operating window might be between 8 A. M. and 8 P. M., Monday through Friday.

Table 1.2 *Uptime and Downtime for a 12x5x52 System*

Availability	Minimum Expected Hours of Uptime	Maximum Allowable Hours of Downtime During Normal Operating Window	Remaining Hours
99%	3088	32	5642
99.5%	3104	16	5642
99.95%	3118	2	5642
100%	3118	0	5642

This table shows that for the 12x5x52 system, there are 5642 hours of remaining time, which can be used for planned maintenance operations that require the system to be down. Even in these environments, *unplanned* downtime must be carefully managed.

Calculating Mean Time Between Failures

Availability is related to the failure rates of system components. A common measure of equipment reliability is the mean time between failures (MTBF). This measure is usually provided for individual system components, such as disks. Measures like these are useful, but they are only one dimension of the complete picture of HA. For example, they do not take into account the differences in recovery times after failure.

MTBF is given by the formula shown in Figure 1.5.

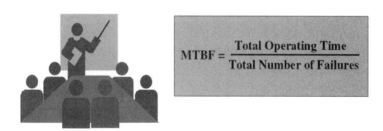

$$MTBF = \frac{\text{Total Operating Time}}{\text{Total Number of Failures}}$$

Figure 1.5 *Mean Time Between Failures*

The MTBF is calculated by summing the actual operating times of all units, including units that do not fail, and dividing that sum by the sum of all failures of the units. Operating time is the sum of the hours when the system is in use (that is, not powered off).

The MTBF is a statement of the time between failures of a unit or units. In common applications, the MTBF is used as a statement of the expected future performance based on the past performance of a unit or population of units. The failure rate is assumed to remain constant when the MTBF is used as a predictive reliability measure.

When gauging reliability for multiple instances of the same unit, the individual MTBF figures are divided by the number of units. This may result in much lower MTBF figures for the components in the system as a whole. For example, if the MTBF for a disk mechanism is 500,000 hours, and the MTBF of a disk module including fans and power supplies is 200,000 hours, then the MTBF of 200 disks together in the system is 1000 hours, which means about 9 expected failures a year. The point is that the greater the number of units operating together in a group, the greater the expected failure rate within the group.

Understanding the Obstacles to High Availability

It is important to understand the obstacles to HA computing. This section describes some terms that people often use to describe these obstacles.

A specific loss of a computer service as perceived by the user is called an **outage**. The duration of an outage is **downtime**. Downtime is either planned or unplanned. Necessary outages are sometimes planned for system upgrades, movement of an application from one system to another, physical moves of equipment, and other reasons.

Unplanned outages occur when there is a failure somewhere in the system. A failure is a cessation of normal operation of some component. Failures occur in hardware, software, system and network management, and in the environment. Errors in human judgment also cause failures. Not all failures cause outages, of course, and not all unplanned outages are caused by failures. Natural disasters and other catastrophic events can also disrupt service.

Duration of Outages

An important aspect of an outage is its duration. Depending on the application, the duration of an outage may be significant or insignificant. A 10-second outage might not be critical, but two

19

hours could be fatal in some applications; other applications cannot even tolerate a 10-second outage. Thus, your characterization of availability must encompass the acceptable duration of outages. As an example, many HP customers desire 99.95% availability on a 24x7 basis, which allows 5 hours of downtime per year. But they still need to determine what is an acceptable duration for a single outage. Within this framework, many customers state that they can tolerate single unplanned outages with a duration of no more than 15 minutes, and they can tolerate a maximum of 20 such outages per year. Other customers frequently wish to schedule *planned* downtime on a weekly, monthly, or quarterly basis. Note that allowing for planned downtime at a given level of availability reduces the number or duration of unplanned outages that are possible for the system.

Time Lines for Outages

The importance of HA can be seen in the following illustrations, which show the time lines for a computer system outage following a disk crash. Figure 1.6 shows a sequence of events that might take place when an OLTP client experiences a disk crash on a conventional system using unmirrored disks for data; when the disk crashes, the OLTP environment is unavailable until the disk can be replaced.

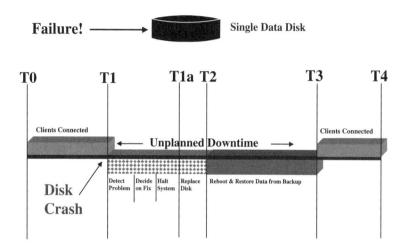

Figure 1.6 *Time Line 1: Unplanned Downtime*

The crash takes place at T1, and the user's transaction is aborted. The system remains down until T3, following a hardware replacement, system reboot, and database recovery, including the restoration of data from backups. This sequence can require anything from a few hours to over a day. In this scenario, the time to recovery may be unpredictable. Downtime is unplanned, and therefore out of the organization's control.

Figure 1.7 shows the same crash when the system uses an HA feature known as disk mirroring, which prevents the loss of service.

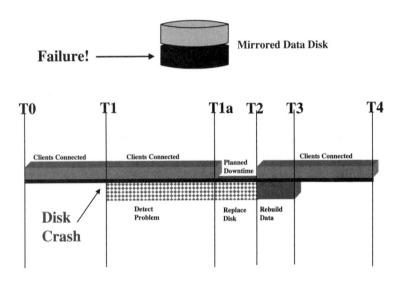

Figure 1.7 *Time Line 2: Planned Downtime*

When the crash occurs, the mirror disk continues to be available, so no data is lost, and service continues. Further, the replacement of the failed disk can be deferred to a period of planned maintenance. A significant difference between this scenario and the preceding one is that you can predict the amount of time needed for the repair, and you can plan the replacement for the least inconvenient time. With disk mirroring, an unpredictable amount of unplanned downtime is replaced by a shorter known period of planned downtime.

A third scenario, shown in Figure 1.8, includes a disk array with hot-swappable disks. This configuration eliminates all downtime associated with the disk failure. (Similar results can be obtained with HA disk enclosures that allow hot plugging of mirrored individual disks.)

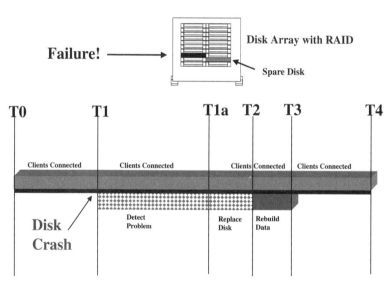

Figure 1.8 *Time Line 3: Downtime Eliminated*

When the crash occurs, a spare disk takes over for the failed mechanism. In this case, the disk array provides complete redundancy of disks, and the failed disk may be replaced by hot plugging a new disk mechanism *while the system is running*. After the replacement disk is inserted, the array returns to the state it was in before the crash.

Causes of Planned Downtime

Planned outages include stopping an application to perform a scheduled backup or to install a software patch. Some others include:

- Periodic backups
- Software upgrades
- Hardware expansions or repairs
- Changes in system configuration
- Data changes

These outages do not normally cause problems if they can be scheduled appropriately. Some data processing environments can tolerate very little planned downtime, if any. Most can tolerate, and plan for, a regular down period every day or week.

An alternative to planned downtime is to carry out maintenance and other system operations while the system is on-line. Backup operations while the system is running are known as **on-line backups**. Hardware upgrades or repairs while the system is running are known as **hot-plug operations**.

Causes of Unplanned Downtime

The following are some common causes of unplanned outages:

- Hardware failure
- File System Full error
- Kernel In-Memory Table Full error
- Disk full
- Power spike
- Power failure
- LAN infrastructure problem
- Software defect
- Application failure
- Firmware defect
- Natural disaster (fire, flood, etc.)
- Operator or administrator error

As far as severity is concerned, an unplanned service outage has a far greater negative impact on the enterprise than a planned outage.

Severity of Unplanned Outages

The effects of unplanned outages include customers waiting in line during a computer crash, airplanes unable to take off or land because of an air traffic control failure, an assembly line coming to a halt, doctors unable to obtain patient data from a hospital information system, and so on. In many cases, business is lost because transactions cannot be completed. An unplanned outage most often reduces customer satisfaction.

Figure 1.9 helps to define the total size of the problem. This figure shows the results of a 1998 Gartner Group survey that measured the causes of unplanned service outages.

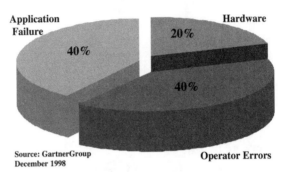

Figure 1.9 *Causes of Unplanned Service Outages*

Traditionally, most people think only of hardware when they think of HA requirements. But as this survey shows, there are other major factors that must be considered when trying to design and implement a true HA environment within your enterprise. The categories of software and people (system and network management) must be factored into this requirement. There are also external elements such as electric and telecommunications services, climate, and weather that must be considered.

Designing for Reaction to Failure

High availability computer systems are designed to eliminate or minimize planned and unplanned outages. In any HA system, it is important to understand the different types of possible failures and how the system will respond to them. Not all outages are caused by failures, but failures will definitely cause outages unless you take steps to intercept them.

Identifying Points of Failure

Availability can be seen as a chain of services that must remain unbroken. Failures are breaks in the chain. The weak links are known as **points of failure**. For each link in the chain that is a possible point of failure, you can reduce the chance of outage by providing a backup or alternate link. This process is called **eliminating points of failure** in the system. The next chapter, "Clustering to Eliminate Single Points of Failure," describes this process in some detail.

Preparing Your Organization for High Availability

Often, the greatest obstacle to HA computing is not a hardware or software failure, but a lack of process. In many respects, HA is a mindset as well as a technology, so the human dimension of the HA system will always be the source of additional failure points. Therefore, it is essential to develop an organization that sees HA as the main priority and that has the skills to cope with the demands of the HA environment. A few suggestions are offered here. In addition, consulting services can assist in carrying out the necessary adjustments in organization that will make the move to HA successful for you.

Identifying Peak Demands and Potential Loss of Availability

In the Internet world of e-vailability, you need to estimate the type of demand your system will be subjected to. Web site demand can grow rapidly, even suddenly, as many startups have discovered, so the system must be capable of rapid and sustained growth in response to the demand. Here are some questions to ask:

- What is the expected initial demand for the system?
- How can the demand be controlled?
- What is the maximum possible demand for the market?
- What is the expected rate of growth in the demand?

Planning should include guidelines for expanding service to meet increased needs as they occur.

Stating Availability Goals

To begin with, it is important to state availability goals explicitly. A service level agreement (SLA), negotiated with the users of the system, is a way of explicitly stating availability requirements in terms of services that are provided to clients within your organization. The SLA can state the normal periods of operation for the system, list any planned downtime, and state specific performance requirements.

Examples of items that appear in SLAs include:

- System will be 99.5% available on a 24x5x52 basis.
- Response time will be 1-2 seconds for Internet-connected clients except during incremental backups.
- Full backups will take place once each weekend as planned maintenance requiring 90 minutes.
- Incremental on-line backups will be taken once a day during the work week with an increase in response time from 2 to 3 seconds for no more than 30 minutes during the incremental backup.
- Recovery time following a failure will be no more than 15 minutes.

The SLA is a kind of contract between the information technology group and the user community. Having an explicit goal makes it easier to see what kind of hardware or software support is needed to provide satisfactory service. It also makes it possible to identify the cost/benefit tradeoff in the purchase of specialized HA solutions.

Note that the system architecture will be different for a large back-end database server than for a system of replicated Internet servers that handle access to a Web site. In the latter case, the use of multiple alternate server systems with sufficient capacity can provide the necessary degree of e-vailability.

Building the Appropriate Physical Environment

Achieving HA requires some attention to the physical data processing environment. Since even small outages are not acceptable, it is important to control as much of this environment as possible so as to avoid problems with overheating, cable breakage, and physical jostling of the system. In addition, highly available systems should be physically secure, possibly under lock and key, and available by login only to authorized personnel.

Creating Automated Processes

Human intervention is always error-prone and unpredictable. Therefore, it is good policy in developing an HA organization to automate as many processes as possible. The following are good candidates for automation through scripts:

- Routine backups
- Routine maintenance tasks
- Software upgrades
- Recoveries following failures

The exact content of scripts for each of these processes will vary, but the use of automation will help prevent outages in the first place, and help restore service as quickly as possible when an outage occurs. In particular, recovery processes should be scripted and rehearsed so that the minimum time will be required when recovery is necessary.

Another important use of automation is in the monitoring of processes that run on the HA system. Monitor scripts or programs can detect problems early and signal the need for corrective action. In some cases, a monitor script can be designed to initiate corrective action on its own, leaving a log message describing the action that was taken. When software is designed to facilitate monitoring in this way, the likelihood of a software failure decreases. Specialized software tools can also provide monitoring and early detection of problems.

Using a Development and Test Environment

When rolling out a new software module that is to run on a highly available system, it is critical to give the module a trial in a test environment before installing it. This avoids the significant risk of disrupting the HA system if the new component brings the system down. In other words, the HA system must be well insulated from software that is untested or is of unknown quality.

Maintaining a Stock of Spare Parts

Another useful tactic in maintaining an HA system is to keep on hand a stock of spare parts that can serve as replacements when hardware failures occur. This stock might include disk mechanisms, power supplies, LAN cards and other network components, and a supply of cables.

Purchasing Capacity on Demand

Another aspect of HA through the use of redundant components is **capacity on demand**. This is essentially a marketing model in which a system is delivered to you with extra capacity, but you pay only for the capacity you use. Then if you develop a need for more memory, additional system processor units (SPUs), or more LAN or I/O capacity, you can enable them simply by entering a lockword. Capacity on demand thus reduces the downtime associated with adding components.

Defining an Escalation Process

When a problem occurs, system administrators and operators must know how to decide on a course of action. This means knowing:

- When automated recovery is taking place
- When a system failure requires action by an operator or administrator
- When a support call is required
- When disaster recovery is necessary

Planning for Disasters

A final aspect of organizational planning for HA is to develop a clear strategy for dealing with a natural or man-made disaster. Under the pressure of a catastrophe, having a scripted, tested procedure ready to execute at a damaged site or at a remote recovery site can make a big difference in the organization's ability to recover.

Training System Administration Staff

System administrators must be trained to think in terms of HA, since the procedures used in the HA environment are frequently different from those for conventional systems. Administrators and operators also need special training to recognize and take correct action swiftly in the event of a component failure. This is especially important since failures are not common, and the "lights out" environment of many HA installations means that a system administrator may not experience a problem very frequently.

Using Dry Runs

One way of providing training is to conduct dry runs or rehearsals of recovery scenarios — simulating a problem and then walking through the solution on the development system.

Documenting Every Detail

Not least in importance in developing an HA environment is to document every detail of the hardware and software configuration and to create a procedures document that is periodically updated and reviewed by system administration staff. Whenever anything in the configuration is added or modified—including hardware components, software modules, and operator procedures—it should be recorded in this document.

Another important document that should be maintained and frequently reviewed is a log of all exceptional activity that takes place on the HA system. This log can include system log file entries. It should also include a list of what corrective actions are taken on the system, by whom, with dates and times. Most importantly, the time required to return service should be carefully recorded for every failure that results in downtime. Planned downtime events may also be logged.

The Starting Point for a Highly Available System

A highly available system is built on top of highly reliable components. HP's enterprise-class servers have the following features, which are the first requirements for components that are to be made highly available:

- Basic hardware reliability
- Software quality
- Intelligent diagnostics
- Comprehensive system management tools
- Maintenance and support services

High availability is not guaranteed by these features, but together they improve the overall availability of the system.

Basic Hardware Reliability

The best way to deliver HA is never to fail in the first place. HP has made a significant investment in designing and manufacturing extremely reliable components for its systems. This results, of course, in highly reliable servers. However, standard reliability will not alone meet the availability requirements of a mission-critical application. For example, all disk drives, being mechanical, go through a life cycle that eventually ends in device failure: no disk will perform forever. Therefore, specific HA storage solutions like disk arrays or disk mirroring are crucial to maintaining HA.

Software Quality

Software quality is another critical factor in the overall scope of HA and must be considered when planning a highly available processing environment. The presence of a software defect can be every bit as costly as a failed hardware component. Thus, the operating system, middleware modules, and all application programs must be subjected to a rigorous testing methodology.

Intelligent Diagnostics

Sophisticated on-line diagnostics should be used to monitor the operating characteristics of important components such as the disks, controllers, and memory, and to detect when a component is developing problems. The diagnostic can then proactively notify the operator or the component vendor so that corrective maintenance can be scheduled long before there is a risk of an unplanned service outage. These intelligent diagnostics improve overall availability by transforming unplanned downtime into planned maintenance.

Comprehensive System Management Tools

System and network management are other major areas that need to be considered for minimizing outages. This is not a criticism of operators, but an acknowledgment of the complexity of today's computing environments. We are now building extremely complex networks that are difficult to manage without automated tools. A single small operator mistake can lead to serious outages.

An integrated set of system and network administration tools such as those provided on HP's OpenView platform can reduce the complexities of managing a multi-vendor distributed network. By automating, centralizing, and simplifying, these tools can significantly reduce the complexity of management tasks. Some tools also have the ability to detect and automatically respond to problems on systems, thus eliminating downtime. Chapter 3, "High Availability Cluster Components," describes some of these tools in more detail.

Maintenance and Support Services

Over time, it will become necessary to upgrade software and hardware components. Also, no matter how reliable a system is, components do fail. For these reasons, it is important to establish hardware and software support contracts with the suppliers of your system components. HP provides a large variety of support levels, including several that are specifically designed for HA users. Consulting is also available during all the phases of deploying an HA system.

Moving to High Availability

Starting with conventional, highly reliable systems, you can obtain HA in several ways:

- By providing redundancy of components
- By using software and hardware switching techniques
- By carefully planning all scheduled downtime
- By eliminating human interaction with the system
- By defining automatic responses to error conditions and events
- By using comprehensive acceptance tests
- By defining and practicing operator responses to unplanned outages that are not handled by automatic response

The use of redundant components eliminates single points of failure in a system, allowing a spare component to take over as needed. Software and hardware switching are what allow a spare component to replace a failed component. In addition, the HA system should attempt to avoid or reduce application outages for planned maintenance; if planned outages cannot be avoided, their duration should be minimized.

Eliminating human interaction allows you to create deterministic responses to error conditions: the same error condition always results in the same system response. The use of networked monitoring tools also lets you automate responses to errors.

Any proposed HA design should be thoroughly tested before being placed in production.

> **NOTE:** If you are really concerned about HA, there is no room for compromise. The upper-most goal must be meeting the HA requirements, and other considerations, such as cost and complexity, take second place. It is important to understand these tradeoffs.

Summary

A highly available system must be designed carefully on paper. It is important to do the following *in the order specified*:

1. Define a goal for availability, including a detailed listing of your service level objectives for each application or service.
2. Identify the maximum duration of an acceptable outage.
3. Measure the availability of the current system, if one is in use. This includes understanding current statistics on availability, including planned and unplanned downtime. Be sure to use measurements consistently, and make sure everyone understands what the measure-

ments mean. Identify all the single points of failure in the current system.

4. Assess your applications. What improvements or changes in availability are desired? What are the costs involved?

5. In conjunction with the next two steps, choose an architecture for HA. More information on this subject follows in Chapter 2.

6. Purchase and configure HA component hardware and software and obtain support services.

7. Create or modify application software.

8. Choose system administration tools.

9. Design processes to be followed in the event of a failure.

10. Document these processes.

11. Train administrators and operators on these processes, and conduct dry runs to prove they work.

12. Document and record the state of the system.

13. Review existing processes on a regular basis.

14. Enforce a change management policy.

The following chapters can help you create an HA design. The emphasis will be on enterprise cluster solutions, which provide the redundancy and switching capabilities that are needed. In addition, HP Consulting can offer assistance in carrying out the analysis, architecting the environment, and choosing the appropriate HA cluster solution for your needs.

CHAPTER 2
Clustering to Eliminate Single Points of Failure

*H*ow do you implement highly available computing? One extremely effective method is the use of **clusters**—networked groups of individual computers. HP's enterprise clusters are loosely coupled host systems—servers running HP-UX, Linux, or Windows—that are especially tailored for HA.

This chapter shows how you can create an HA cluster by configuring redundant groups of highly reliable hardware and software components together with HA software in such a way as to eliminate single points of failure. In addition, the chapter discusses single-system HA in both clustered and non-clustered solutions.

Here is what will be covered:

- Identifying Single Points of Failure
- Eliminating Power Sources as Single Points of Failure

- Eliminating Disks as Single Points of Failure
- Eliminating SPU Components as Single Points of Failure
- Eliminating Single Points of Failure in Networks
- Eliminating Software as a Single Point of Failure
- Implementing a High Availability Cluster

Note that most of the specific solutions described in this chapter were introduced originally on HP-UX systems, and some of them are not available on all platforms. Over time, however, it is expected that HA clusters in Linux and Windows will provide many of the same features that are provided in HP-UX. As of this writing, HP's Linux cluster implementation was moving toward its first release, and the Windows version was in the design phase.

Identifying Single Points of Failure

A highly reliable stand-alone system still has many single points of failure. A **single point of failure** (SPOF) is a hardware or software element whose loss results in the loss of service. Usually, a component that is not backed up by a standby or redundant element becomes an SPOF.

Consider a typical client/server installation on a single system as shown in Figure 2.1. Clients—that is, applications running on a PC or UNIX workstation—connect over the network to a server application that is executing on the SPU. The server application reads and writes records on behalf of the clients; these

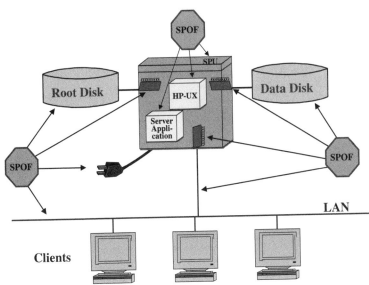

Figure 2.1 Single Points of Failure in a Reliable System

records are stored on the data disk. The operating system, located on the root disk, handles client connections, data transfer, memory allocation, and a host of other functions on behalf of the executing application.

What can go wrong in this scenario? Here are just a few examples of potential problems:

- The system goes down because of a failure in a CPU card.
- The LAN cable is damaged, or a LAN card fails, and clients lose service.
- Following a system reboot, an operator restarts an application in the wrong mode, and clients cannot connect.

43

- A media failure on the root disk causes the system to go down.
- A media failure on the data disk causes data loss and interruption of service.
- A power failure results in a system reboot and loss of data.
- The operating system runs out of file space or swap space.

Typical failures of these components are shown in Table 2.1, together with a description of how the SPOF can be eliminated.

Table 2.1 *Eliminating Single Points of Failure*

Component	What Happens If Component Fails	How the SPOF Is Eliminated
Single SPU	Service is lost until the SPU is repaired.	Provide a backup SPU to the host application. For example, create a cluster of host systems.
Single LAN	Client connectivity is lost.	Install redundant LAN interface cards and subnets. Configure stand-alone interfaces.
Single LAN Interface	Client connectivity is lost.	Install redundant LAN interface cards, or configure standby LAN interfaces in a grouped net.
Single Root Disk	Service is lost until disk is replaced.	Use mirrored root disk.

Table 2.1 *Eliminating Single Points of Failure (Continued)*

Component	What Happens If Component Fails	How the SPOF Is Eliminated
Single Data Disk	Data is lost.	Use mirrored storage for individual disks or use disk arrays in data protection mode.
Single Power Source	Service is lost until power is restored.	Use additional power sources, and employ UPS technology on each.
Single Disk Interface Card (e.g., Fast/Wide SCSI)	Service is lost until card is replaced.	Use dual or redundant Fast/Wide SCSI cards with a dual I/O path to a disk array configured with LVM.
Operating System (OS)	Service is lost until OS reboots.	Provide failover capability, and tailor applications to restart and recover.
Application Program	Service is lost until application restarts.	Provide a facility to restart the application automatically. Tailor applications to restart and recover. Provide careful, thorough debugging of code.
Human Being	Service is lost until human error is corrected.	Automate as much operation as possible. Document manual procedures thoroughly.

The following sections show in more detail how you can eliminate SPOFs in a stand-alone system as you create a simple HA cluster.

Eliminating Power Sources as Single Points of Failure

Figure 2.1 showed all the components in the system connected to a single power source. This is a very obvious point of failure, which can be corrected in a number of ways. The use of multiple power circuits with different circuit breakers reduces the likelihood of a complete power outage. An uninterruptible power supply (UPS) provides standby power in the event of an interruption to the power source. Small local UPS units can be used to protect individual SPUs and data disks. Larger power passthrough units can protect the power supply to an entire computer system.

Individual UPS Units

Small individual UPS units function by switching to battery power for a short period after a power failure. This allows processing to continue until power comes back or until a graceful shutdown can be carried out. A small UPS can protect a few system components, but remember that the UPS itself can also fail, and this can cause a system outage even when several individual UPS units are used to protect different parts of the system.

Figure 2.2 shows devices connected to two different circuits. The dotted lines show which devices are protected by each UPS. Smaller installations may find the use of individual UPS

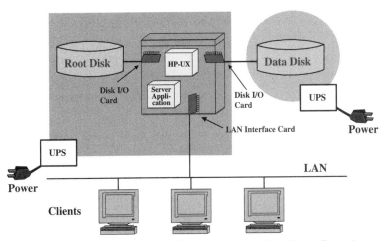

Figure 2.2 *Conventional System Using Multiple Circuits*

technology adequate to protect the integrity of the system during a short power failure. For instance, the UPS should provide power for enough time that the system can cleanly commit or back out all queued transactions, synchronize all logs, and gracefully shut itself down.

Power Passthrough UPS Units

A more complete (and more expensive) method for providing redundant power is the use of power passthrough UPS units. A power passthrough UPS does not itself become an SPOF because it is designed to simply pass the power through until a power failure, at which point the loss of inductance closes a switch and initiates battery backup. This larger UPS can be employed to provide battery backup power for all the units connected to a large electrical service panel. The UPS unit can also be wired to provide power from a generator that starts up when normal electric service fails. Figure 2.3 shows a power passthrough UPS protecting an entire system. The large arrow represents the power source.

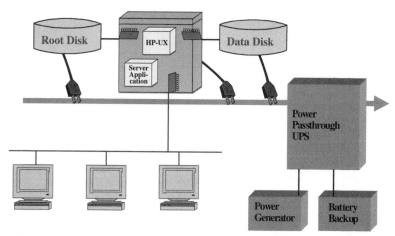

Figure 2.3 *System Protected by Power Passthrough UPS*

Eliminating Disks as Single Points of Failure

Another obvious SPOF is the disks in a conventional reliable system. In Figure 2.1, two disks were shown: the root disk and a data disk. If there is a media failure on the root disk, the system may be unable to continue normal processing. The disk must be replaced and its contents replaced by reinstalling system software and/or restoring data from backups.

If the data disk fails in a conventional reliable system, the system may remain up, but application processing will stop until a new disk can be installed and the data recovered. For either root or data disk failure, the system must be rebooted and the data restored from backups. In this case, data will be lost between the time of the last backup and the time of the media failure.

Redundancy is necessary to prevent the failure of disk media or a disk controller from causing an outage to users. There are two methods available for providing disk redundancy: using disk arrays in a redundant configuration and using software mirroring. Each approach has its own advantages.

Data Protection with Disk Arrays

One technique for providing redundant data storage is the use of disk arrays in RAID configurations that provide data protection. The acronym RAID stands for *redundant array of inex-*

pensive disks. A group of disks functions together in a variety of configurable arrangements known as RAID levels. Some levels allow hardware mirroring, while others provide protection through the use of parity data, which allows the array to reconstruct lost data if a disk mechanism fails.

Common RAID levels are as follows:

- RAID 0: The controller writes data to all disks in stripes. This level provides no data protection.
- RAID 1: The controller writes data to mirrored groups of disks.
- RAID 3: Data is striped byte-wise, and the controller stores parity information on a separate disk so that lost data from any disk can be recovered.
- RAID 5: Data is striped block-wise, and the controller spreads parity information across all disks so that lost data from any disk can be recovered.

In addition, you can configure arrays in independent mode, which means that each member of the array is seen as an independent disk.

Some advantages of using disk arrays for protected data storage are as follows:

- Easy on-line replacement of a failed disk spindle.
- Capability of assigning a hot standby spindle to take over for a failed spindle.
- Highest storage connectivity (multiple terabytes).
- Flexibility in configuration (different modes available).

- Potential for high performance in small I/O size read-intensive environments.
- On some devices, dual controllers, power sources, and fans can eliminate SPOFs.

Figure 2.4 shows a sample configuration.

NOTE: In Figure 2.4, the root disks are also shown as mirrored. Software mirroring is further described in the next section.

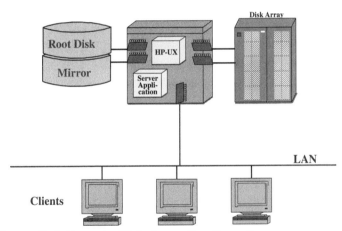

Figure 2.4 *Sample Disk Array Configuration*

Data Protection with Software Mirroring

An alternative technique for providing protected data storage is the use of software mirroring, which is an implementation of RAID 1 on individual disks. Mirroring is frequently implemented through software products. In HP-UX, software mirroring is done using Logical Volume Manager (LVM) and the separate MirrorDisk/UX subsystem, or by using the Veritas VxVM volume manager. In Linux and Windows, a variety of different hardware and software techniques for mirroring are available from different vendors.

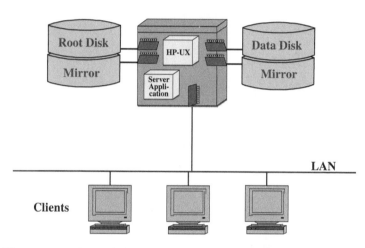

Figure 2.5 *Sample Mirrored Disk Configuration*

Figure 2.5 shows a primary and a mirror copy of the data disk. Note that the mirror copy is shown on a separate I/O bus. This arrangement eliminates the disk, the I/O card, and the bus as SPOFs. If one disk is lost, the other continues operating with no interruption in service. Note that the root disks are also mirrored.

The failed disk must, of course, be replaced. This can be done at a period of planned downtime when the system can be brought down. Some configurations even allow **hot plugging**, which means replacement of components while the system is up, or **hot swapping** of disks, which means replacement while the application is still running. These options reduce or eliminate planned downtime.

Mirroring through software has several advantages:

- Two- or three-way mirroring is possible. Additional mirror copies can be configured with the Veritas VxVM volume manager.
- Mirror copies can be split off for backup, perhaps on another system.
- There is the potential for better performance from the use of multiple read paths, multiple disk controllers, and multiple disk spindles.
- Each disk has its own controller, so the loss of one disk tray or tower does not prevent access to the data.
- There is control of data placement for better application performance tuning.
- You can take advantage of the mirrors being configured on different FibreChannel or SCSI buses to "double" the I/O rate to a given data area.
- An individual disk controller is not a bottleneck.

Mirrors should be powered from different sources.

Protection Through Storage Area Networks

A storage area network (SAN) is an approach to storage that separates disk devices from individual systems by attaching storage through a special network that is dedicated to storage. In configurations of this kind, the SAN is designed for high availability, and it can be attached to the system via a highly available high-speed network. Individual components of the SAN, such as storage controllers and individual disk arrays, must be configured in HA modes. A conceptual view of a SAN is shown in Figure 2.6. More information, including examples of HA configuration for SANs, is given in Chapter 6.

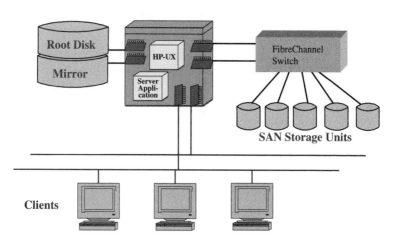

Figure 2.6 SAN Configuration

Eliminating SPU Components as Single Points of Failure

A system processor unit, or **SPU,** in an HP 9000 system consists of a group of elements, any of which can fail. The most important are:

- One or more central processing units (CPUs)
- I/O controllers
- Memory boards

If one of these components fails, the system typically undergoes a reboot, after which a system start-up test will map out any failed components. Thus, even a stand-alone system has a degree of availability provided by this self-diagnosis. However, the loss of service during this reboot time may be unacceptable. Moreover, the system must eventually be brought down for repairs, and this means additional downtime.

There are two ways of eliminating SPOFs in an SPU:

- Use stand-alone systems with redundant SPU components.
- Use HA clusters.

Creating a Highly Available Standalone System

A growing number of high-end systems today provide redundant components within a single box. These include:

- Processors
- LAN interface cards
- I/O cards
- Memory components
- Power supplies and connectors
- Hardware partitions

Very high-end servers like the HP 9000 SuperDome configurations provide hardware cells that operate much like single systems. Cells can be swapped in or out as needed, and they can be combined into one or more partitions, each of which runs its own instance of the operating system.

An advantage of a system like the SuperDome is capacity on demand, which lets you swap in additional components and pay for them at the time they are deployed. Another feature is extensive diagnostic monitoring by Hewlett-Packard with call-home capability. This kind of monitoring makes it possible to detect upcoming failures before they occur and replace components proactively.

> *NOTE:* There are still SPOFs in many high-end systems with hot-pluggable components: some bus components cannot be made redundant, and a single system clock may be used to coordinate the entire system.

An example of a highly available single system is an SD-class system configured with four partitions. This configuration is shown in Figure 2.7.

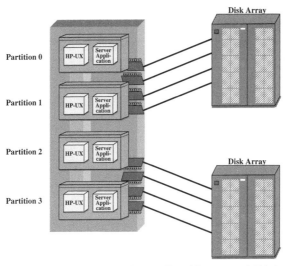

Figure 2.7 *SD Series with Four Partitions and Disk Arrays*

Using Clusters to Eliminate Points of Failure

The use of cluster architecture also lets you eliminate the SPU as an SPOF. A cluster eliminates or significantly reduces the downtime associated with an SPU failure, allowing you to repair or replace failed components without losing service. In an HA cluster, one or more systems acts as a backup to the SPU(s) of the system on which the application primarily runs. These backup systems can be either active or standby systems. Active systems run their own applications while serving as the backup for another system. Standby systems may be idle until a failover occurs, or they can be used for other processing. Clustered systems are flexible, and for some applications, they are more cost-effective than highly available single systems such as the Super-Dome. A simple clustered system with two nodes is shown in Figure 2.8.

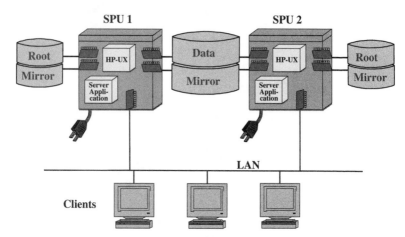

Figure 2.8 *Two-Node Cluster Providing Redundant SPUs*

Note the distinction between node and SPU. The SPU is a system processor unit containing one or more central processing units (CPUs), memory, and a power supply. A **node** is a host system, which is a member of a cluster. The SPU is a component within the node. The two nodes are connected to each other by a local area network (LAN), which allows them to accept client connections and transmit messages that confirm each other's health. If one node's SPU should fail, the other node can restart the application after only a brief delay, in a process known as

failover. After the failover, clients can access applications running on the second node as easily as they accessed those applications on the first node.

The process of failover is handled by special HA software running on all nodes in the cluster. Different types of clusters use different cluster management and failover techniques. The specific differences in cluster types and their HA software are described in more detail in Chapter 3, "High Availability Cluster Components."

Note that the data disks are physically connected to both nodes so that data is also accessible by the other node in the event of failover. Each node in a cluster has its own root disks, but each node may also be physically connected to several other disks in such a way that multiple nodes can access the data. On HP systems, this cluster-oriented access is provided by the Logical Volume Manager (LVM). Access may be exclusive or shared, depending on the kind of cluster you are creating. All disks that are intended for cluster use must be connected to the primary node and to all possible alternate nodes.

Eliminating Single Points of Failure in Networks

In cluster networks, as with the other parts of an HA cluster, it is important to eliminate SPOFs. Therefore, the network should use redundant components. Wherever possible, network hardware should be configured with monitors that allow error detection and reporting.

Networks are configured and used in clustered systems for two main purposes:

- Access to an application by clients or other systems
- Communication between cluster nodes

These are treated separately in the next sections.

Points of Failure in Client Connectivity

In a conventional system, the LAN is used for client connection to the server application. The entire communication link from the client system to the application server system is subject to failures of various kinds. Depending on the type of LAN hardware, failures may occur in cables, interface cards, network routers, hubs, or concentrators. There may also be failures in networked software systems such as Domain Name Services (DNS). This is a case where the failure of a remote system (the

DNS server) can prevent clients from connecting to an application, even when the local system that hosts the application is up and running.

Example Points of Failure

Figure 2.9 shows a simple picture of one type of LAN configuration that provides connectivity to clients.

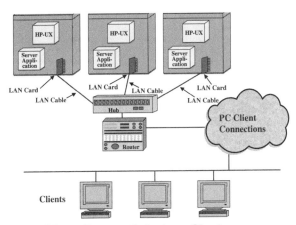

Figure 2.9 *Client Connectivity to a Cluster*

The figure shows an Ethernet star topology connecting three cluster nodes to a router, which provides access to the cluster from outside. Using this kind of configuration, clients can connect to individual nodes, and nodes can communicate with one another. However, the configuration shown in Figure 2.9 is *not* highly available; some of the SPOFs in the configuration are shown in Figure 2.10.

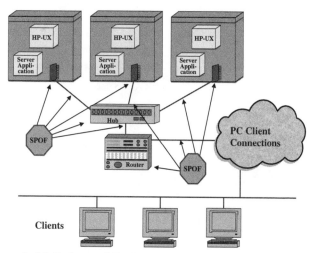

Figure 2.10 *Points of Failure in LAN Configuration*

All of the following are points of failure in the configuration shown in Figure 2.10:

- Client systems
- Router
- Ethernet hub
- Cables
- LAN interface cards

At the cluster end, failures may occur in cables and LAN interface cards. Of course, a client PC can fail, but this does not constitute an SPOF in the cluster, since other clients can still connect, and the user can move to another client system.

Points of Failure in Inter-Node Communication

In a cluster, the HA software establishes a communication link known as a **heartbeat** among all the nodes in the cluster on a subnet known as the **heartbeat subnet. Heartbeat messages** allow the HA software to tell if one or more nodes has failed. This special use of networking must itself be protected against failures. Points of failure in the heartbeat subnet include the LAN interfaces and cables connected to each node.

Eliminating the Failure Points

You can eliminate single points of network failure in two major ways:

- Providing fully redundant LAN connections
- Configuring local switching of LAN interfaces

Providing Redundant LAN Connections

To eliminate cable failures, you can configure redundant cabling and redundant LAN interface cards on each node. To eliminate the loss of client connectivity, you can configure redundant routers through which clients can access the services of the cluster. In a redundant configuration, the loss of one router does not mean that connectivity is lost. You can also configure redundant hubs to protect against hub failure. Figure 2.11 shows a configuration that has eliminated SPOFs in the network.

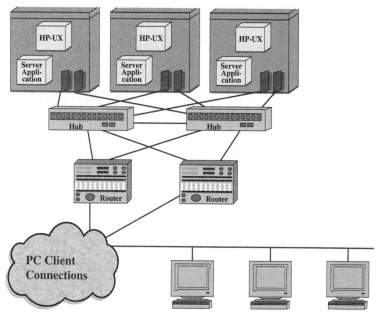

Figure 2.11 Highly Available Network Configuration

In some configurations, you cannot eliminate all points of failure. For example, when clients are connected directly to a LAN segment, the loss of that segment means that no clients can connect.

Configuring Local Switching of LAN Interfaces

Another way to eliminate points of failure is to configure local switching, which means shifting from a configured LAN interface card to a standby when network connectivity is lost. This may happen if the cable is cut or unplugged or if the LAN card itself fails. Local switching is only possible if you configure standby LAN interfaces for each node. These standbys must be on the same **grouped subnet** as the primary interfaces. A grouped subnet is a domain of physical connectivity; it consists of multiple LAN segments connected by a bridge. Both active and standby segments are available to support the same subnet in the event of a switch.

The connector between the segments can be of different types, depending on the type of LAN system. Examples are:

- A bridge that supports the spanning tree protocol
- Two Ethertwist hubs interconnected with each other

How IP Addresses Are Handled

An interface that currently has an IP address associated with it is known as a **primary interface**; an interface that does not currently have an IP address associated with it but is connected to the same subnet as the primary is known as a **standby interface**. Local switching of LAN interfaces requires moving the node's IP addresses from the active to the standby interface. When the software detects a primary interface failure, it will switch the IP addresses from the failed interface card to a healthy standby interface card, which then becomes the new primary.

Examples of Redundant LAN Configuration

A few illustrations show some of the effects of LAN redundancy in a cluster. A simple configuration is shown in Figure 2.12.

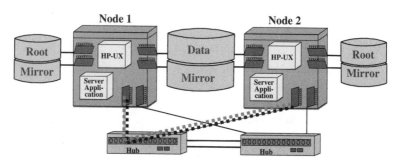

Figure 2.12 *Ethernet LANs in a Grouped Subnet*

In the figure, a two-node cluster has one grouped subnet configured with both a primary and a standby LAN card on each node. The grouped subnet is being employed for the user connections as well as for the heartbeat. Data is shown passing between the two nodes using the primary interface on each node.

What happens in a failure scenario? Suppose the primary LAN card fails on Node 2. Then the HA software switches Node 2's IP address to the standby interface on Node 2 and data continues to flow, now passing across the bridge and through the standby (now primary) interface on Node 2. The new state is shown in Figure 2.13.

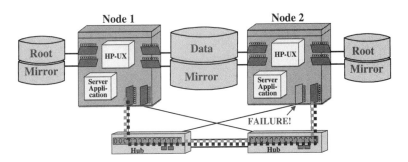

Figure 2.13 Grouped Net After Card Failure

Figure 2.14 shows the state of the grouped net following a LAN cable break. In this case, the primary LAN interface on Node 1 switches to the standby, which is connected to a good cable and is therefore able to communicate with the other node.

In some cases, you might wish to use a second grouped subnet. This can be useful if LAN traffic is expected to be heavy.

Another alternative is to configure redundant active LAN interfaces for inter-node communication. In this case, the failure of any one interface or cable segment does not interrupt service.

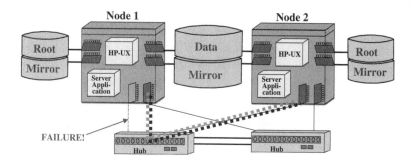

Figure 2.14 *Grouped Net Following LAN Cable Failure*

Automatic Port Aggregation

Another technique for achieving redundant LAN connectivity is the use of **automatic port aggregation** (APA), a special networking product that is available with recent versions of HP-UX. (A similar technology in Linux is called **trunking**.) This technology aggregates multiple fast Ethernet or Gigabit Ethernet ports, including the ports on different cards, into a logical link aggregate that uses a single IP address. This allows automatic fault detection and recovery, as well as load balancing among the physical links. Automatic port aggregation is shown in Figure 2.15.

Providing Redundant FDDI Connections

If you are using FDDI, you can create a redundant configuration by using a star topology to connect all the nodes to two concentrators, which are also connected to two routers, which

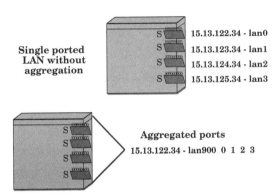

Figure 2.15 *Automatic Port Aggregation*

communicate with the world outside the cluster. In this case, you use two FDDI cards in each node. The configuration is shown in Figure 2.16.

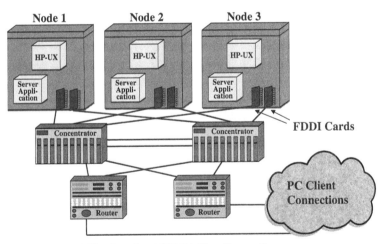

Figure 2.16 *Redundant FDDI Configuration*

69

Using Dual-Attached FDDI

Another way of obtaining redundant LAN connections is to use dual-attached FDDI cards to create an FDDI ring, shown in Figure 2.17. An advantage of this configuration is that only one slot is used in the system card cage.

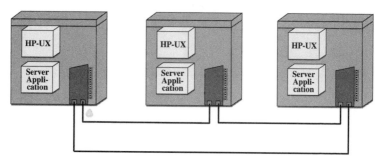

Figure 2.17 *Dual-Attached FDDI Configuration*

The use of dual-attach cards gives protection against failures in both cables and connectors, but does not protect against card failures. LAN card failure would result in the application's switching to another node. (This process is described in a later section, "Eliminating Software as a Single Point of Failure.")

Redundancy for Dialup Lines, Hardwired Serial Connections, and X.25

Dialup lines, hardwired connections, and X.25 links are typically attached to a system with a direct physical connection. In an HA environment, these links will typically be unavailable during a failover episode. Special design must occur to include these links in a failover.

The solution for dialup lines and hardwired serial connections is the same: move these lines and connections from the computer system to an intermediate data communications terminal controller (DTC). Upon recognizing a failure to respond by the primary host interface, the DTC would reconnect the dialup lines and hardwired serial connections to the backup system. To prevent the DTC from becoming an SPOF, configure additional DTC units and segment your users.

Providing redundancy for X.25 links is more difficult, since specialized programming may be required. For switched virtual circuits, redundancy is achieved via software included by the X.25 provider. For permanent virtual circuits, X.25 expects a physical link to terminate in a unique X.121 address. In this case, one solution is to use controllers with a dual-ported connection panel (such as ACC). The panel can be controlled by two computer systems and permits ports to be switched between the two systems when failures occur. This solution requires special coding in the failover scripts.

More on Highly Available Networking

Many of today's enterprises are large, and are often distributed over wide geographic areas with trans-continental or global scope. For these businesses, long-distance clustering presents special challenges in the area of networking. Without a highly available connection from client to server, various points of failure can disrupt service. The greater the distance, the more opportunities for points of failure.

Therefore, a highly available network needs to eliminate points of failure in a number of different layers within the network fabric, as shown in Figure 2.18.

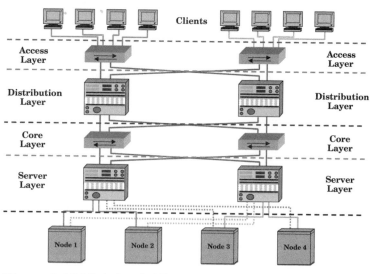

Figure 2.18 High Availablility Network Layers

Access Layer

The *access layer* (wiring closet) handles the client connectivity to the access layer switch. Not every client may be connected to more than one access layer switch, but multiple switches are provided so that a client can change to a different switch in case of a failure.

Distribution Layer

The *distribution layer* provides a switch for aggregating high-speed access from the access layer. Each switch at the access layer is connected to multiple switches at the distribution layer.

Core Layer

The *core layer* switch (network backbone) is interfaced to the upstream distribution layer and to the downstream server layer. There must be multiple connections in both directions.

Server Distribution Layer

The *server distribution layer* switch (data center switch) handles the server connectivity to the network switch within the LAN. Each server must be connected to LAN segments that are attached to different data center switches.

Network Availability Tracking

Network availability tracking is provided by special monitoring software (known as the Foundation Monitor) that is included with the Enterprise Cluster Master Toolkit product (a set of tools for implementing specific solutions with HA clusters). A daemon monitors the availability of networking connections by sending ping packets every 30 seconds from the server nodes to each of the access layer switches. This process verifies the continuous availability of network communication across the entire network on every node in the cluster.

A successful return of a packet marks the access layer switch status as up for the availability of network connectivity. If a packet is not returned, then ping packets are sent to each client node that is associated with the access layer switch. If one of the client nodes responds, then the access layer switch status is marked as up for the availability of network connectivity. If none of the client nodes respond, then the access layer switch status is marked as down for inaccessible network connectivity.

The access layer switch status can be recorded in log files whenever a down event occurs. For example, if the access layer switch status changed during the previous 24 hours, a summary report is generated. The following sample from a summary report shows the status for the network switch named netsw1:

```
Network Name:        netsw1
IP Address:          192.11.11.100
Start Down Time:     Aug 19, 1999 08:12:24
Start Up Time:       Aug 19, 1999 08:13:19
```

Tools such as the network Foundation Monitor make it possible to determine exactly the degree of HA your system has achieved. If problems occur, their consequences can be quantified.

Wide Area Networks

Creating HA configurations using wide area network (WAN) technology poses a new set of problems. HP's basic cluster technology requires a LAN. But for distances greater than 100 km (60 miles), a WAN is necessary to provide communication links for enterprise servers and their clients. One solution is to create groups of clusters in a configuration known as a **continental cluster**, which is essentially two separate local clusters (each on its own LAN) that communicate with each other over WAN links. Continental clusters are described in detail in Chapter 5, "Disaster-Tolerant High Availability Systems." Another possible solution is the 5nines:5minutes remote mirroring technology described in Chapter 6. As networking technology develops further, additional solutions are sure to emerge.

Wide area networking itself has special HA issues. For example, most users of wide area networking employ leased lines from common carriers. These lines must be configured redundantly to eliminate SPOFs. It may be necessary to rely on the common carrier to provide the redundant connections. Note, however, that requesting a second line may not be sufficient if the carrier routes both lines through the same physical cable. There may be two different subnets, but there is still one SPOF.

DWDM

For long-distance optical communication, carriers in many countries are providing access via Dense Wave Division Multiplexing (DWDM) technology. Using DWDM, a group of signals are transmitted together over the same high-speed fiber optic cable, permitting a sharing of bandwidth at reduced cost. In using DWDM or other long-distance services provided by common carriers, it is important to understand whether redundant signals are being transmitted over separate physical cables or whether they are being routed to different portions of the bandwidth of a single cable. In the latter case, the cable is still a SPOF.

Eliminating Software as a Single Point of Failure

Many software components are susceptible to failure. These include:

- Operating system (OS)
- Database server software
- Transaction processing (TP) monitors
- Server applications
- Client applications

The use of clusters can prevent the worst effects of many of these failures. For example, if there is an OS failure, the node shuts down, and services that were on the failed node are made available on another system in the cluster. One way to do this is to have another node take over the applications that were running on the failed system. In this approach, the application is seen as a **package** of services that can move from node to node as needed.

Another approach is to provide different instances of the same application running on multiple nodes so that when one node goes down, users only need to reconnect to an alternate node. In both cases, the use of clusters makes recovery from failure possible in a reasonably short time.

Failures are also possible in database server software and transaction monitors. To eliminate SPOFs, these components can be made highly available by incorporating them into packages.

Also common are failures of server applications. In the event of an application failure, the cluster must be able to restart or reset the application or run it on another available SPU. It is the job of HA software monitors to determine when a failure has occurred.

Finally, failures are possible at the client level as well. Therefore, client software should be designed for automatic restart and reconnection to the server where possible.

Tailoring Applications for Cluster Use

After eliminating SPOFs, it is important to make application programs operate correctly in an HA environment. In developing an HA environment, application programs must be created or tailored especially for cluster use. This means designing applications with the following characteristics:

- Ability to fail over to another node
- Ability to restart automatically, without operator intervention

- Support for user connections on any node, not a particular host
- Monitoring functions for determining whether the application is up or down
- Well-defined startup and shutdown procedures
- Well-defined backup, restore, and upgrade procedures

Many off-the-shelf applications can be used in HA clusters without major changes; others require you to create specialized monitoring tools. Guidelines for coding applications to run effectively in the HA environment are included in the user's guides for individual HA software products.

In developing applications for HA use, be sure to carefully document the startup, shutdown, backup, restore, and upgrade procedures for operators and administrators. Special training in HA procedures also ensures that you will experience the least possible downtime.

Implementing a High Availability Cluster

A **high availability cluster** is a grouping of servers having sufficient redundancy of software and hardware components that a failure will not disrupt the availability of computer services. The result of eliminating SPOFs in power, disk, SPU, networking, and software is a true HA cluster, as shown in Figure 2.19.

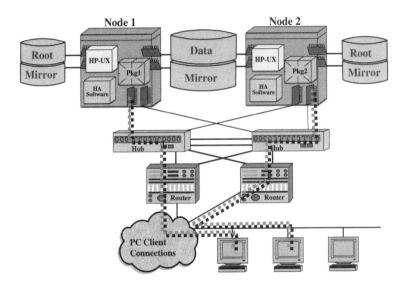

Figure 2.19 *High Availability Cluster*

In this composite figure, we see a two-node configuration with a two-LAN grouped subnet and mirrored individual root and data disks. Application programs run as part of the packages on each node. If there is a failure of a component on one node, the package may start up on the other node, as shown in Figure 2.20.

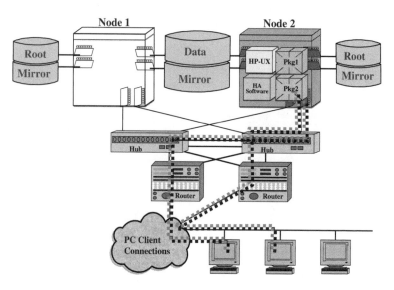

Figure 2.20 *High Availability Cluster After Failover*

The task of implementing this cluster is a fairly straightforward process of configuring hardware and software components. The details vary somewhat, depending on the components you select. Most of the products described in the rest of this book were developed to support this fairly simple cluster model.

Although there are differences in the way different kinds of failover behavior are implemented, the cluster configuration itself remains common to all HA cluster types.

Complete High Availability Solution

To develop a complete HA solution, you need to maintain HA within a hierarchy of system levels, some of which go beyond the cluster level. Failures at all levels must be detected quickly and a fast response provided. At the same time, planned maintenance events at all levels must be possible with minimal disruption of service. Table 2.2 shows a hierarchy of system levels where HA planning is necessary.

Table 2.2 *Levels of Availability*

System Level	How High Availability Is Achieved
Hardware Component Level	Redundant components and/or switching techniques must be provided.
Firmware Level	Error correction must be incorporated.
Server (Host) Level	SPU must be redundant; dual I/O paths to the data must be provided.
Operating System Level	Mirroring of system software must be implemented.
System and Network Management Level	Distributed system administration and network monitoring tools must be made highly available.

Table 2.2 *Levels of Availability (Continued)*

System Level	How High Availability Is Achieved
Cluster Level	Data must be protected. Communication among nodes must be highly available. There must be multiple nodes capable of running applications.
Database Level	Database must be capable of starting up on a different node or must run on more than one node at the same time.
Transaction Processing (TP) Level	Transaction monitors and all the services they use must be highly available.
Application Level	Applications must be robust and capable of recovering from errors. Applications and/or TP monitors must be capable of switching to another processor and restarting without operator intervention.

CHAPTER 3
High Availability Cluster
Components

*T*he previous chapters described the general requirements for HA systems and clusters. Now we provide more detail about a group of specific cluster solutions provided by Hewlett-Packard. Topics include:

- Nodes and Cluster Membership
- HA Architectures and Cluster Components
- Other HA Subsystems
- Mission-Critical Consulting and Support Services

The solutions described here have been implemented under HP-UX, and many of them have already been ported to Linux, with ports to the Microsoft Windows environment expected shortly.

Nodes and Cluster Membership

HP's clustering solutions are all designed to protect against data corruption while providing redundancy for components and software. To achieve these goals, the individual nodes in a cluster must communicate with each other to establish and maintain a running cluster group. This is accomplished partly through two important cluster properties:

- Heartbeats
- Cluster quorum

Heartbeats

Heartbeats are the means of communicating among cluster nodes about the health of the cluster. One node that is designated as the **cluster coordinator** sends and receives messages known as heartbeats from the other nodes in the cluster. If heartbeat messages are not sent and received by a certain node within a specific (user-definable) amount of time, the cluster will re-form itself without the node.

Heartbeats can be carried on more than one LAN. Then, if there is a problem with one LAN, the heartbeat can be carried on the other LAN. Figure 3.1 shows heartbeat configured for a simple two-node cluster.

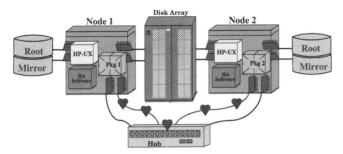

Figure 3.1 *Cluster Heartbeat*

When the heartbeat is lost between cluster nodes, the result is a cluster re-formation, and if one node is unable to communicate with a majority of other nodes, it removes itself from the cluster by causing itself to fail, as shown in Figure 3.2. This failure, known as a Transfer of Control (TOC), is initiated by the cluster software to ensure that only one application is modifying the same data at any one time.

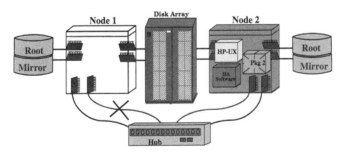

Figure 3.2 *Loss of Cluster Heartbeat*

Cluster Quorum

Under normal conditions, the cluster software monitors the health of individual nodes while applications are running on them. If there is a node failure, the cluster re-forms in a new configuration without the failed node. If there is a communication failure between two sets of nodes, then the set with the greater number of nodes (more than 50%) will be allowed to form a new cluster. This greater number is known as the **cluster quorum**. If the two sets of nodes are of equal size, then both will try to re-form the cluster, but only one can be allowed to succeed. In this case, a **cluster lock** is used.

Cluster Lock

The cluster lock provides a tie-breaking capability in case a communication failure leads to a situation where two equal-sized groups of nodes are both trying to re-form the cluster at the same time. If they were both to succeed in forming new clusters, there would be a "split brain" situation in which the two clusters would access a single set of disks. If this were to happen, data corruption could occur. "Split brain" is prevented by requiring a group of nodes to acquire the cluster lock. The successful group re-forms the cluster; the unsuccessful nodes halt immediately with a TOC. The cluster lock is sometimes implemented as a lock disk, which is a part of an LVM volume group that is used to indicate ownership of the cluster. Figure 3.3 shows a lock disk that has been acquired by one node after a cluster partition.

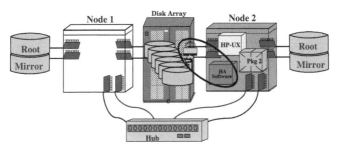

Figure 3.3 *Cluster Lock Acquired by Node 2*

Quorum Server

An alternative to a cluster lock disk is a **quorum server**, which is a software process running on an independent system that provides the tie-breaker when two equal-sized sets of nodes are competing to form a cluster. The quorum server is required in the Linux implementation, but it is available on HP-UX as well. Figure 3.4 shows an example of a quorum server. The quorum server cannot run in the same cluster for which it is providing the tie-breaker, but it can run as a highly available package in another cluster. (Packages are described in detail later in this chapter.)

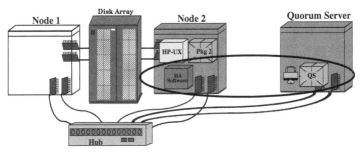

Figure 3.4 *Quorum Server as Tie-Breaker*

The main point of the cluster quorum rule—whether implemented as a lock disk or as a quorum server—is to prevent data corruption that might occur if more than one node tried to run the same application and modfy the same logical volumes. The cluster architectures described throughout the rest of this book have been carefully designed so as to eliminate SPOFs while also eliminating the possibility of data corruption.

HA Architectures and Cluster Components

The cluster shown so far in this book is a generic, loosely coupled grouping of host systems. In fact, each SPU can be connected to another SPU in a variety of highly available cluster configurations. Three basic types are:

- **Active/standby configuration**—one in which a standby SPU is configured to take over after the failure of another SPU that is running a mission-critical application. In an active/standby configuration, two or more SPUs are connected to the same data disks; if one SPU fails, the application starts on the standby. The failed system can then be serviced while the application continues on the standby system. In the active/standby configuration, the backup node may be idle or it may be running another less important application. HP's ServiceGuard product provides active/standby capability.

- **Active/active configuration**—one in which several nodes may be running mission-critical applications, and some can serve as backups for others while still running their own primary applications. HP's ServiceGuard product also provides active/active capability.

- **Parallel database configuration**—a cluster in which the different nodes each run separate instances of the same database application and all access the same database concurrently. In this configuration, the loss of a single node is not critical since users can connect to the same application running on another node. HP's ServiceGuard OPS Edition product provides the parallel database implementation for use with Oracle Parallel Server.

The following sections describe HP's implementations of each of these cluster architectures.

Active/Standby Configurations Using ServiceGuard

A flexible active/standby configuration which allows the application to start on the standby node quickly, without the need for a reboot, is provided by ServiceGuard. Figure 3.5 shows a two-node active/standby configuration using ServiceGuard. Applications are running on Node 1, and clients connect to Node 1 through the LAN. It is also possible to configure a cluster in which one node can act as a standby for several other nodes.

High Availability Cluster Components

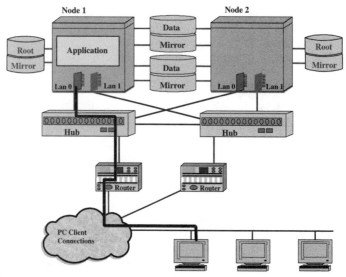

Figure 3.5 *Active/Standby Cluster Before Failover*

In this configuration, the first node is running the application, having obtained exclusive access to the data disks. The second node is essentially idle, though the operating system and the HA software are both running.

The state of the system following failover is shown in Figure 3.6.   After failover, the applications start up on Node 2 after obtaining access to the data disks. Clients can then reconnect to Node 2.

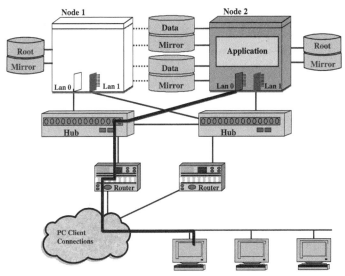

Figure 3.6 *Active/Standby Cluster After Failover*

Note that a failure is not necessary for a package to move within the cluster. With ServiceGuard, the system administrator can move a package from one node to another at any time for convenience of administration. Both nodes remain up and running following such a voluntary switch.

The primary advantage of an active/standby configuration is that the performance of the application is not impaired after a switch to the standby node; all the resources of the standby node are available to the application.

Active/Active Configurations Using ServiceGuard

In an active/active configuration, two or more SPUs are physically connected to the same data disks, and if there is a failure of one SPU, the applications running on the failed system start up again on an alternate system. In this configuration, application packages may run on all nodes at the same time. Figure 3.7 shows a two-node active/active configuration before the failure of one host. Different applications are running on both nodes.

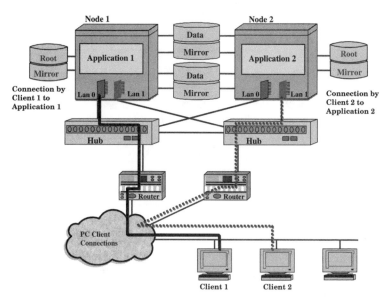

Figure 3.7 *Active/Active Cluster Before Failover*

Figure 3.8 shows an active/active configuration following the failure of one host. The second node still carries on with the applications that were previously running, but it now also carries the application that was running on Node 1 before the failure.

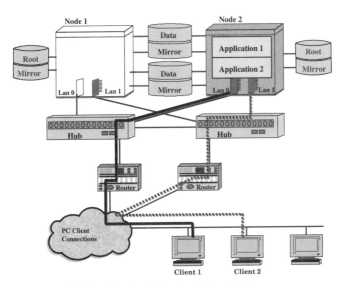

Figure 3.8 *Active/Active Cluster After Failover*

In an active/active configuration, ServiceGuard does not use a dedicated standby system. Instead, the applications that were running on the failed node start up on alternate nodes while other packages on those alternate nodes continue running.

Parallel Database Configuration Using ServiceGuard OPS Edition

In a parallel database configuration, two or more SPUs are running applications that read from and write to the same database disks concurrently. Special software (Oracle Parallel Server, or OPS) is needed to regulate this concurrent access. In the event one cluster node fails, another is still available to process transactions while the first is serviced. Figure 3.9 shows a parallel database configuration before the failure of one node.

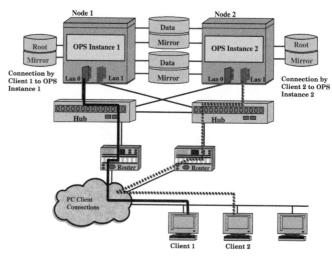

Figure 3.9 *Parallel Database Cluster Before Failover*

Figure 3.10 shows the parallel database cluster after the failure of one node. The second node remains up, and users now may access the database through the second node.

94

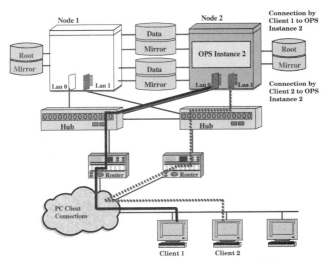

Figure 3.10 *Parallel Database Cluster After Failover*

How ServiceGuard Works

Applications, together with disk and network resources used by applications, are configured in **packages,** which can run on different systems at different times. Each package has one or more application **services** which are monitored by ServiceGuard; in the event of an error in a service, a restart or a failover to another node may take place. A particular benefit of Service-Guard is that you can configure failover to take place following the failure of a package, or following the failure of individual services within a package. You can also determine whether to try restarting a service a certain number of times before failover to a different node.

With ServiceGuard, there need not be any idle systems; all of the nodes can run mission-critical applications. If one node fails, the applications it supports are moved and join applications that are in progress on other nodes.

Under normal conditions, a fully operating ServiceGuard cluster simply monitors the health of the cluster's components while the packages are running on individual nodes. Any node running in the ServiceGuard cluster is called an **active node**. When you create a package, you specify a **primary node** and one or more **adoptive nodes**. When a node or its network communications fails, ServiceGuard can transfer control of the package to the next available adoptive node.

The primary advantage of the active/active configuration is efficient use of all computing resources during normal operation. But during a failover, performance of applications on the failover node may be somewhat impacted. To minimize the impact of failover on performance, ensure that each node has the appropriate capacity to handle all applications that might start up during a failover situation.

Use of Relocatable IP Addresses

Clients connect via the LAN to the server application they need. This is done by means of IP addresses. The client application issues a `connect()` call, specifying the correct address. Ordinarily, an IP address is mapped to an individual hostname—that is, a single HP-UX system. In ServiceGuard, the IP address is assigned to a package and is temporarily associated with whatever host system the package happens to be running on. Thus, the client's **connect()** will result in connection to the application, regardless of which node in the cluster it is running on.

Figure 3.11 shows a cluster with separate packages running on each of two nodes. Client 1 connects to a package by its IP address. The package is shown running on Node 1, but the client need not be aware of this fact.

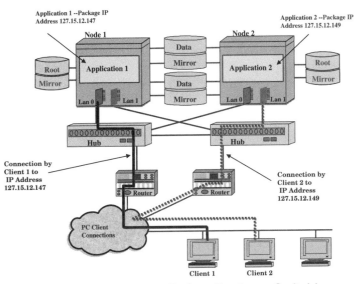

Figure 3.11 *IP Addresses Before Package Switching*

After a failure on Node 1, the package moves over to Node 2. The resulting arrangement of packages is shown in Figure 3.12. Note that the IP address of the package is the same.

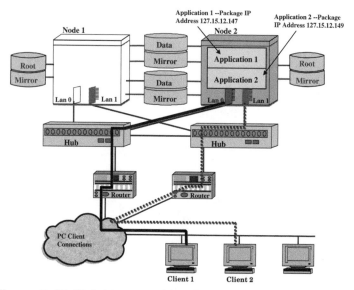

Figure 3.12 *IP Addresses After Package Switching*

The key benefit of using relocatable IP addresses with packages is transparency. The client is unconcerned with which physical server is running a given application. In most cases, no client or server code changes are needed to take advantage of relocatable IP addresses.

Application Monitoring

Central to the functioning of ServiceGuard is the monitoring of user applications. When a package starts, its applications are started with a special cluster command that continues to monitor the application as long as it is running. The monitor immediately detects an error exit from the application, and alerts ServiceGuard. Depending on the kind of error condition, Service-Guard can restart the application, halt the application, or fail it over to a different node.

Fast Recovery from LAN Failures

ServiceGuard monitors the status of the LANs used within each node of the enterprise cluster. If any problem affects the LAN, ServiceGuard will quickly detect the problem and activate a standby LAN within the same node. This detection and fast switch to an alternate LAN is completely transparent to the database and attached clients. This feature eliminates the downtime associated with LAN failures and further strengthens the enterprise cluster environment for supporting mission-critical applications.

Workload Balancing

The use of application packages provides an especially flexible mechanism for balancing the workload within the cluster after a node failure. Individual application packages within a single node can be moved to different alternate nodes, distributing the workload of one node across the surviving nodes of the cluster. For example, a cluster with four nodes is configured and each node is running three packages. If a node fails, each of the three packages running on that node can be moved to different nodes. This distributes the workload of the failed node among all of the remaining nodes of the cluster and minimizes the performance impact on the other applications within the cluster.

This same package capability also allows the workload of a cluster to be balanced according to the processing demands of different applications. If the demand of one application package becomes too high, the system administrator can move other application packages on the same node to different nodes in the cluster by using simple commands, thus freeing processing power on that node for meeting the increased demand.

Workload tuning within individual nodes of an enterprise cluster can be further refined by using HP's Process Resource Manager (HP PRM), described in a later section.

Failover Policy and Failback Policy

Added flexibility in the cluster workload configuration is provided by the ability to choose a failover policy for packages. You can choose to fail a package over to the node with the fewest packages currently running on it, or you can have it fail over to a specific node whatever its load.

You can also control the way packages behave when the cluster composition changes by defining a failback policy. If desired, a package can be set up in such a way that it fails over to an adoptive node and then fails back to the original node as soon as the original node becomes available again.

Figure 3.13 shows a cluster with a package failing over to an adoptive node, then failing back to its original node.

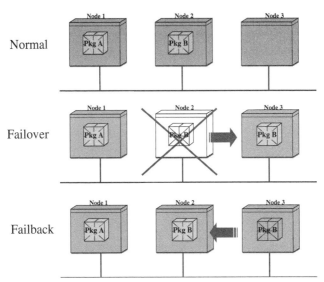

Figure 3.13 *Failover and Failback Policies*

Rolling Upgrades

Another useful feature of ServiceGuard is the ability to upgrade the software on a given node—including the OS and the HA software—without bringing down the cluster. You carry out the following steps for every node in the cluster:

1. Move applications from the node that is to be upgraded to some other node in the cluster.
2. Remove the node from the cluster.
3. Perform the upgrades.
4. Allow the node to rejoin the cluster.
5. Move applications back to the upgraded node.

When using this feature of ServiceGuard, you must carefully plan the capacity of the nodes in the cluster so that moving an application from one node to another during upgrades will not degrade performance unacceptably.

How ServiceGuard Works with OPS

ServiceGuard OPS Edition is a special-purpose HA software product that allows host servers to be configured with Oracle Parallel Server (OPS), which lets you maintain a single database image that is accessed by the HP 9000 servers in parallel, thereby gaining added processing power without the need to administer separate databases. Oracle Parallel Server is a special relational database design that enables multiple instances of the Oracle database to function transparently as one logical database. Different nodes that are running OPS can concurrently read from and write to the same physical set of disk drives containing the database.

Oracle Parallel Server handles issues of concurrent access to the same disk resources by different servers and ensures integrity of Oracle data.

The OPS Edition uses the same underlying cluster mechanism as basic ServiceGuard. This means that you can create and manipulate packages as well as OPS instances on the cluster. Note the following difference, however: In basic ServiceGuard, packages run on only one node at a time, whereas in the OPS Edition, OPS applications may run concurrently on all nodes in the OPS cluster.

Fast Recovery from LAN Failures

Like ServiceGuard, ServiceGuard OPS Edition monitors the status of the LANs used within each node of the OPS cluster. Problem detection and fast switching to an alternate LAN is completely transparent to the database and attached clients.

Protecting Data Integrity

When a node fails, ServiceGuard OPS Edition instantly prevents the failed node from accessing the database. This capability prevents a hung node or a node that has rebooted itself after a failure from inadvertently (and incorrectly) attempting to write data without coordinating its actions with the other node (this situation, which was described previously, is called split-brain syndrome).

Reduced Database Administration Costs

OPS clusters can also help reduce administrative costs through the consolidation of databases. In networks that employ multiple independent databases or partitions of the database on different nodes, an OPS cluster can substantially reduce database administration costs by allowing the multiple databases to be consolidated into one logical database. Even though two nodes are accessing the database from within the cluster, the database is managed as a single unit.

Oracle Parallel FailSafe

A new cluster design from Oracle is known as Oracle Parallel FailSafe. Parallel FailSafe is built upon OPS running in a primary/secondary configuration. In this configuration, all connections to the database are through the primary node. The secondary node serves as a backup, ready to provide services should an outage at the primary occur. Unlike OPS, Parallel FailSafe is tightly integrated with HP clustering technology to provide enhanced monitoring and failover for all types of outages.

Parallel FailSafe can support one or more databases on a two-node cluster. All databases are accessed in a primary/secondary mode, where all clients connect through a single instance on one of the nodes. In a primary/secondary configuration, only one server, the primary, is active at any time. The secondary is running an Oracle instance, but that instance is not doing any work. During normal operations, clients are connected to the primary instance using a primary IP address. In addition, they can be pre-connected to the secondary instance using a secondary IP address.

The result of integrating ServiceGuard OPS Edition with Oracle Parallel Failsafe is the simplicity of traditional cluster failover in which the database and applications run on only one node in the cluster. This is important because it means the solution works with no code changes for all types of third-party applications that are designed to work with a single instance of Oracle, but are not parallel server-aware. In addition, the Parallel FailSafe solution provides much faster detection and bounded failover in the event of a failure, with improved performance after failover thanks to pre-connected secondary connections and a pre-warmed cache on the secondary node.

An example showing a single primary instance is depicted in Figure 3.14.

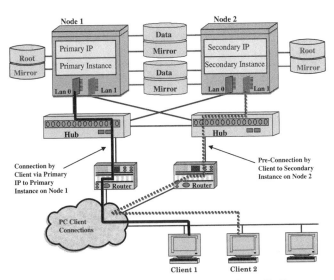

Figure 3.14 *Oracle Parallel FailSafe Before Failover*

After failover, the failover node starts up the primary instance, as shown in Figure 3.15.

Failover time depends on a number of factors in Service-Guard clusters, including the time it takes to obtain a cluster lock, the time required for running startup scripts on the failover node, and the database recovery time required before transactions can

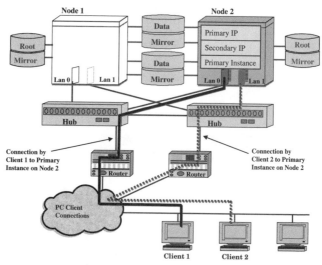

Figure 3.15 *Oracle Parallel FailSafe After Failover*

be processed on the failover node. Oracle Parallel FailSafe can reduce this recovery time significantly. In addition to the standby Oracle instance, other applications can run on the standby node. Note also that on a cluster with more than two nodes, each node can run an instance of Oracle 8i that may fail over to the standby node.

Disaster-Tolerant Architectures

Many of the cluster designs presented so far in this chapter can be extended and adapted for use in long-distance and wide area environments as well. Such clusters are known as disaster-tolerant clusters because they protect against the kinds of events that affect entire data centers, sometimes even entire cities or regions. Examples are natural disasters like hurricanes.

Three types of modified architecture have been developed based on the standard ServiceGuard cluster:

- Campus cluster
- Metropolitan cluster
- Continental cluster

These types are described fully in Chapter 6.

Other HA Subsystems

To help you further enhance the overall availability, flexibility, and ease of management of your mission critical environment, the following products and services are suggested:

- Software mirroring
- Automatic port aggregation (APA)
- HA disk enclosure
- HP disk arrays
- HP SureStore Disk Array XP Series
- EMC disk arrays
- Enterprise Cluster Master Toolkit
- NFS Toolkit

- ServiceGuard Extension for SAP
- Journaled file system (JFS)
- OnLineJFS
- Veritas Volume Manager
- Transaction processing (TP) monitors
- PowerTrust uninterruptible power supplies (UPS)
- System management tools

Each of these is described further below.

Software Mirroring

Basic mirroring of individual disks is provided with MirrorDisk/UX. Operating through the HP-UX Logical Volume Manager (LVM), MirrorDisk/UX transparently writes data to one primary volume and up to two mirror volumes. By mirroring across different disk adapters (channels), MirrorDisk/UX provides protection against the failures of all major components associated with data.

An added benefit of MirrorDisk/UX is the capability for on-line backup. The mirror is "split" from the primary, resulting in a static copy of the data that is used for a backup. After the backup is performed, MirrorDisk/UX will transparently handle the resynchronization of the mirror and primary data. In cases where you need the highest levels of protection, three-way mirroring allows the on-line backup function to be performed while the primary disk is still being mirrored.

Software from Veritas Corporation also provides extensive mirroring capability for logical volumes. Veritas VxVM is an alternative volume manager provided on HP-UX 11i and later systems; and CVM (described below) provides mirroring support for HP-UX clusters.

Automatic Port Aggregation

Autoport aggregation (APA), available as a separate product on HP-UX 11.0 and later systems, allows you to group multiple physical fast Ethernet or Gigabit Ethernet ports into a logical link aggregate. Once enabled, each link aggregate can operate as a single logical link with only one IP and MAC address. This technology provides automatic fault detection and recovery for HA as well as increased bandwidth with load balancing among the physical links.

High Availability Disk Storage Enclosure

Conventional disk mechanisms may be mounted in a special HA storage enclosure that permits hot plugging, that is, removal and replacement of one disk in a mirrored pair without loss of service while the OS is running and the device is powered on. HP-UX system administration is required during the replacement to allow the old disk to be removed from the mirrored group and to allow the new disk to be added back to the mirrored group.

High Availability Disk Arrays

HP's HA disk array products provide an alternate method of protecting your vital application data. These are hardware RAID units that can be configured so that all major components are redundant, including not just the disk drives, but also the power supplies, fans, caches, and controllers. The dual controllers can both be used simultaneously from the server to read and write volumes on the array, improving performance as well as enhancing availability. If any major component fails, the redundant component picks up the workload without any loss of service. Furthermore, the repair of the failed component does not require any scheduled downtime for maintenance. All the major components are hot-swappable, that is, they can be replaced on-line.

These units also support a global spare for the disk volumes. This means that one spare drive unit can be used as a backup of all the RAID volumes that have been configured in the array. If one drive fails in any of the defined volumes, the global spare is used to quickly re-establish full redundancy.

HA disk arrays support RAID 0 (striping), RAID 1 (mirroring), RAID 0/1 (striping and mirroring), and RAID 5 (rotating parity). They support up to 64MB of read/write cache per controller. Drives can be added on-line, up to the maximum system capacity.

HP SureStore Disk Array XP Series

The HP SureStore Disk Array XP Series offers large data capacity together with many enhanced HA features. This array provides full redundancy of components, including power supplies, fans, disk mechanisms, processors, and caches.

The XP Series lets you define storage units (LUNs) for use on individual systems and cluster nodes. Raid Manager software provides additional capabilities: Business Copy allows you to split off duplicate volumes for off-line backup or other purposes; and Continuous Access lets you establish and maintain links to other XP arrays for physical data replication. These capabilities underlie the physical data replication used in specialized metropolitan and continental clusters (described further in Chapter 5).

EMC Disk Arrays

High-capacity disk arrays are also available from other vendors. A notable example is the Symmetrix product family of cached disk arrays from EMC Corporation. In addition to providing very high capacity, Symmetrix arrays allow connections from the same data disks to multiple cluster nodes across different FibreChannel or SCSI buses.

The Symmetrix EMC SRDF facility, like Continuous Access on the XP Series, allows direct hardware connection to other disk arrays for physical data replication.

Enterprise Cluster Master Toolkit

The Enterprise Cluster Master Toolkit contains a variety of tools for developing HA solutions using ServiceGuard clusters. Individual toolkits included in the Master Toolkit product include:

- Netscape Internet Server toolkit
- Netscape Messaging Server toolkit
- Netscape Calendar Server toolkit
- Oracle toolkit
- Oracle Standby Database toolkit
- Informix toolkit
- Progress toolkit
- Sybase toolkit
- Foundation Monitor toolkit

Each toolkit consists of a set of sample scripts or other tools plus documentation on using it to build a specific HA solution.

A separate NFS toolkit product is also available.

ServiceGuard Extension for SAP R/3

The specialized environment of SAP R/3 requires special customization when implemented in a ServiceGuard cluster. One component, the Enqueue Server, can be made highly available in different ways—by using a standard package arrangement or by building a special component known as Somersault into the application. Somersault maintains parallel state tables on multiple nodes for a crucial SAP service; in the event of failover, this state table remains immediately available on the failover node.

An SAP R/3 configuration is especially complex, and should be implemented by specialists in SAP and ServiceGuard configuration. Consulting services are available specifically for this configuration.

Journaled File System

The journaled file system (JFS), a standard feature of HP-UX, is an alternative to the UNIX high-performance file system (HFS). JFS uses a special log to hold information about changes to file system metadata. This log allows JFS to improve availability by reducing the time needed to recover a file system after a system crash. With JFS, the file system can be restarted after a crash in a matter of seconds, which is much faster than with HFS.

As JFS receives standard read/write requests, it maintains an intent log in a circular file that contains file system data structure updates. If a file system restart is performed, `fsck` only needs to read the intent log and finish the outstanding updates to the data structures. Note that this does not normally include user data, only the file system data structures. This mechanism assures that the internal structure of the file system is consistent. The consistency of user data is achieved by a transaction logging mechanism.

OnLineJFS

OnLineJFS is an optional product that adds extensions to JFS. This product eliminates the planned downtime that is associated with typical file system maintenance activities. With OnLineJFS, activities such as defragmentation, reorganization, and file system expansion can all be performed while applications are accessing the data. (The conventional HFS requires that applications be halted before performing these kinds of maintenance activities. HFS does not support or require defragmentation.)

The on-line backup feature is provided by designating a *snapshot* partition. As writes are made to the data, a copy of the old data is copied to the snapshot. This allows applications to access the latest data while the backup process accesses a static copy of the data. The size of the partition needed to hold the snapshot will vary depending on the number of writes performed to the data during the time that the snapshot is maintained; typically, a snapshot will require 2-15% of the disk space of the original data.

Veritas Cluster Volume Manager

With the HP-UX 11i release, the Veritas Volume Manager (VxVM) became a standard software component shipped with all systems. For clusters, a special volume manager known as the Cluster Volume Manager (CVM) offers several important advantages over the earlier LVM provided with HP-UX. LVM requires you to import a volume group separately on each cluster node;

CVM lets you set up a disk group only once and have it immediately visible to all nodes in the cluster. Tools are provided for converting from LVM to CVM disk storage.

Transaction Processing Monitors

Transaction processing (TP) monitors ensure availability in a matter of seconds when used in conjunction with HA clusters by resubmitting transactions to another node when the first node fails. Transaction Processing monitors enable quick restart after any failures and guarantee that incomplete transactions are rolled back. Furthermore, in a mission-critical environment, the TP monitor combines operations of subsystems into one transaction, and integrates the various resources residing in different locales into global transaction services. This ability to globally manage heterogeneous subsystems cannot be achieved by databases alone.

TP monitors available on HP systems include CICS/9000, Encina/9000, TUXEDO, Top End MTS (MicroFocus Transaction System), and UniKix.

Uninterruptible Power Supplies

Installing an HP PowerTrust uninterruptible power supply (UPS) in an HP-UX computer system ensures that power is maintained to your computer, preventing problems such as networking time-outs and tape rewinds. PowerTrust provides at least 15 minutes of continuous backup power, ensuring that data is not lost in the event of a power failure.

A PowerTrust UPS can be configured to bring a system down gracefully before its batteries deplete, thus maintaining data integrity and ensuring a clean reboot and reasonably fast file system recovery. For larger installations, you may wish to use passthrough UPS power protection.

System and Network Management Tools

HP offers a comprehensive set of software tools that allow for centralized, automated management of a wide-ranging network of servers and workstations from many different vendors. See Chapter 5 for complete details.

Mission-Critical Consulting and Support Services

The use of consulting and support services is highly recommended when you are developing an HA system. HP's HA product family encompasses the following consulting and support services:

- Availability management service
- Business continuity support
- Business recovery services

HP has vast experience in creating HA solutions for the UNIX environment, and all HA customers are encouraged to take advantage of this specialized know-how.

Availability Management Service

One main focus of this consulting service is to perform a comprehensive operational assessment of a mission-critical processing environment. This includes analyzing all aspects of the environment such as the hardware being used, software versions and tools, business processes related to the computing environment, as well as the skill set of data processing personnel. This service will identify weaknesses in the processing environment that might cause service outages and will create a plan to eliminate the identified weaknesses.

A second area of consulting is the design and implementation of an availability management plan. Consultants can assist in the following areas:

- Project management
- System and network software installation
- System performance testing
- Full site design, cabling, and testing
- Tuning and enhancement of operations
- Customization, integration, and testing of availability management tools and processes

Business Continuity Support

Business continuity support (BCS) is HP's most comprehensive support offering. It is designed for use in mission critical environments where unacceptable financial or business damage results from even short outages. Business Continuity Support has been crafted to ensure maximum application availability by targeting potential planned and unplanned outages at their source and taking direct action to prevent them or minimize their duration and impact on your business.

The first step in the delivery of BCS is an operational assessment. This is a consulting engagement in which an HP availability expert reviews your system and operations environment, analyzes its strengths, identifies gaps that could lead to outages, and makes recommendations to help you reach your availability goals. Next, a service level agreement (SLA) is developed with you, and your account team of HP experts is identified and made thoroughly familiar with your environment, business, and support needs.

The BCS account team then provides several *proactive* services:

- Change management planning services to carefully plan, script, and assist in changes of any kind to the computing environment.
- Daily review, communication, and planning for applying patches that are appropriate for your environment, or otherwise heading off potential problems.
- Regular technical reviews to advise and convey information on a variety of HA topics.
- Continuous monitoring of your HP system for anomalies that could escalate into outages if action is not taken.

The BCS team also provides *reactive* services in the event of an outage. HP provides a commitment to restoring your business operation in four hours or less, usually a lot less. This commitment is possible because of HP's investment in a large global response infrastructure of tools, resources, and processes, and HP's staff of experienced recovery experts.

Business Continuity Support is delivered with a commitment to an intimate understanding of your business and IT environment, and total care for that environment. BCS complements the other investments you make in HA technology and operations processes, and offers peace of mind for your users.

Network Availability Services

To meet the needs of IT managers and network administrators, HP offers HP network availability services and HP assessment services for networks to extend mission-critical support to the network. These network services can be purchased stand-alone or as a complement to HP critical systems support and BCS to help you realize maximum system and network uptime. Network availability services provide a suite of scalable services that utilize assigned network specialists to provide reactive and proactive support for your network.

Assessment services for networks provide three levels of services to optimize network availability. The assessment services include proactive identification of potential critical points of failure, and analysis and recommendations to optimize network performance and improve operational and IT processes.

Business Recovery Services

Another group of services for HA systems is business recovery services. These services are used to provide protection against disasters and large-scale failures. Business recovery services are discussed in Chapter 6, "Disaster-Tolerant Solutions."

CHAPTER 4
Cluster Monitoring and Management

*T*he use of HA clusters, as we have seen, can eliminate SPOFs and significantly reduce unplanned downtime in the data center. But clustering alone will not eliminate failures altogether. Since components ultimately fail, an important consideration in designing an HA solution is to manage failure events closely. To do this job well, the cluster administrator needs good monitoring and management tools.

The ideal in monitoring and management is to develop a *proactive* approach that attempts to intercept failures before they occur. Monitoring of critical component thresholds with sophisticated tools can often allow you to replace components before they fail. When a failure does occur, a redundant component takes over and continues providing service, but the failed component must now be replaced. And before the component can be replaced, someone must be notified that the failure has taken place and then initiate action to remedy the problem. For example, an HA disk array such as the XP256 can be configured to provide spares that take over when a disk volume goes bad. But the next step is to unplug the bad disk and plug in a good one, bringing the system back to its original state.

This chapter presents a brief introduction to the subject of monitoring, then surveys a variety of tools that help keep the HA environment running smoothly. Topics include:

- Basics of Monitoring
- Event Monitoring Services
- HA Monitors
- Hardware Monitors
- ServiceGuard Manager
- High Availability Observatory
- System and Network Management Products
- ServiceControl Manager

Basics of Monitoring

How is monitoring done? There are several approaches, all of which have their place in monitoring the HA environment. Here are some basic monitor types:

- Hardware indicators: These are used primarily for devices such as disks, networking devices, and interface cards. The design of the device includes a provision for providing state information.
- Software monitors: These indicators provide data from the OS as well as from running applications.

Hardware Indicators

The simplest kind of hardware monitor is a flashing light that indicates the status of a physical device. Disk drives and LAN cards frequently use red or flashing lights to indicate that one or more devices has had a failure. The use of this kind of monitor is extremely simple: someone sees the light, and then takes action.

The problem with this model is that in a large environment with thousands of disk drives, the job of continually monitoring the stock of disks becomes labor-intensive and expensive, not to mention very tedious (someone has to be paid to see if any lights are flashing). This also rules out "lights out" environments where no personnel are physically present.

Figure 4.1 shows an example of the "flashing light" approach on an array of disks, in which one disk develops trouble.

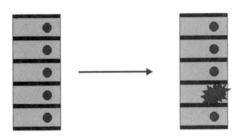

Figure 4.1 *Monitoring via Flashing Lights*

One alternative to observing a flashing light is to have a device send an electrical signal when there is a failure; the computer can then "notice" the signal and notify personnel only when necessary. In this case, the computer does the job of continually monitoring the stock of disks, keeping a table with information about each one, and sending a message when a failure occurs. This type of monitoring is actually a partnership between hardware and software; the OS or monitoring system interprets the meaning of the electrical signals provided by the device. Incidentally, this type of monitoring is not foolproof: The same failure (power supply, for example) might result in the loss of a disk drive as well as the loss of its ability to send an electrical signal. In other words, the monitor can die at the same time as the device itself. An answer to this problem is provided through **polling**, that is, attempting to activate the device at periodic intervals. If the device does not return a response stating that the activation was successful, the device is marked *down*.

Instrumented components are designed to provide information about their own behavior. A simple example of a device with instrumented components is a printer with a diagnostic mode that displays or prints out data about the device itself. More sophisticated hardware monitoring is possible by creating test equipment that interfaces to the device directly and then observing the electrical activity. This kind of monitoring is impractical except in unusual circumstances, such as when engineers are developing and testing the device.

Software Monitors

If the element that is being monitored is an application program—a database, for example—the object might be to determine whether or not the database is experiencing a hang. No hardware monitor would detect this, except as a hard-to-interpret reduction in activity. But a software program could continuously communicate with the database in a very simple way, such as by reading a small table in shared read mode, with an error response showing that the database is not functioning. This kind of monitor can also send a message to a DBA (database administrator) or other administrator

One sophisticated kind of monitor displays maps of devices with state information about each one. This kind of monitor can be designed to emulate the simple flashing light described earlier, by displaying a flashing red icon to indicate a device or system that is in trouble. Examples of this include ClusterView and its successor, ServiceGuard Manager. Both of these are described in some detail later.

Event Monitoring Services

An HA environment requires proactive system administration to keep the components of a cluster running. This means *monitoring the cluster*—carefully observing the behavior of cluster components, and replacing faulty hardware or software as soon as possible. In the simplest terms, monitoring means checking specific information on a system to detect only unusual circumstances within the cluster or one of its parts. In these cases, the **Event Monitoring Service** (EMS) lets you choose the type of monitoring you want to do and decide how the information from monitoring is to be used.

Using Individual EMS Monitors

EMS monitors give you control over the response to particular changes in status, allowing you to send messages that trigger administrative response. The EMS is a framework with the following components:

- Tools for configuring resource monitoring

- A group of different notification methods for sending messages when a resource experiences an unusual event or reaches a critical value
- Easy integration of new EMS resource monitors using a standard application programming interface (API)

The central focus of monitoring is on the **resource**, that is, the thing you are monitoring. Monitors track the occurrence of predefined conditions known as **events** that are considered important within the HA framework. An event could be the failure of a component, loss of availability (that is, detection of an SPOF), or even the gradual degradation of a cluster element that indicates the element should be replaced. Figure 4.2 shows the process at its simplest.

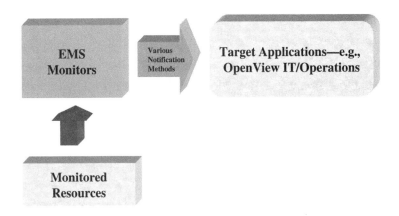

Figure 4.2 *Resources, Monitors, and Targets*

Components of the Event Monitoring Service

The EMS consists of a group of separate components whose job is to manage the reporting on the status of particular resources. These are:

- Monitor applications
- Registry (EMS framework)
- Configuration clients
- Target applications

These components are shown in Figure 4.3 and discussed further in the following paragraphs.

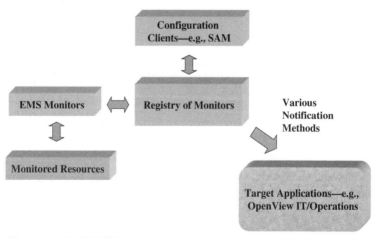

Figure 4.3 *EMS Components*

Monitor Applications

An EMS monitor is an application program that observes the status of a resource over time and notifies the EMS framework when something unusual occurs. The monitor is started up by the framework at specified polling intervals. HP provides monitors with its High Availability Monitors product, with its Event Monitoring Service, and with specific hardware components, including disk arrays, LAN hardware, and memory. In addition, third-party developers provide EMS-compliant monitors to support specific hardware and software products.

Hardware diagnostics are also provided through EMS monitors, to allow users to proactively observe a device's behavior and detect trends that might indicate a failure in the making. Proactive monitoring is especially helpful in eliminating the unplanned downtime that accompanies the need to replace hardware components.

Configuration Clients

Configuration clients are components that let you define monitoring requests. The best example of this is the SAM subarea that is devoted to monitoring EMS resources. One screen from SAM is shown in Figure 4.4.

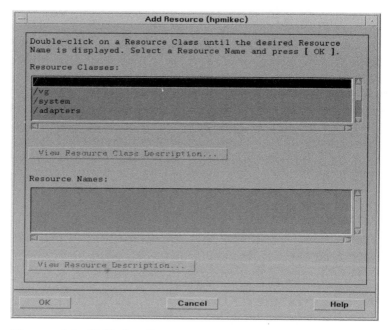

Figure 4.4 *EMS Configuration Client in SAM*

A completed monitoring request identifies the following:

- What resources to monitor
- What events to watch for and how often

- What notifications to send when an event occurs
- Where to send notifications

Events are defined for one of two resource state types:

- Periodic checking against either thresholds or state/value changes
- Continuous checking for asynchronous stateless events

Monitoring requests are stored in the Registry.

Registry (EMS Framework)

The registry, also known as the EMS framework, starts up monitors and provides the interface between the configuration clients, monitor applications, and target applications. When a monitor is installed, it is registered by the creation of a group of entries in a monitor dictionary. As monitoring requests are received from configuration clients (described below), the dictionary expands to include data for each request. When a monitor reports an interesting event, the registry sends messages of the specified type to a target application.

Resource entries in the registry are hierarchical, as Figure 4.5 shows (note that this is not a file system structure).

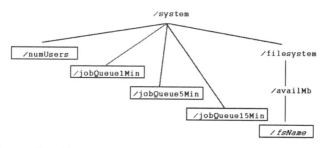

Figure 4.5 *Resource Hierarchy*

A typical system monitor request might be concerned with defining monitoring of the available space in a file system. The configuration client might define monitoring as follows:

```
/system/filesystem/availMB/fsName < 100MB
```

and then indicate where to send notifications (target applications) in case this value is reached.

Target Applications

System administrators use target applications to receive event notifications and possibly take action. The target application can be any application that understands the EMS-supported protocols. The supported message types (protocols) are:

- TCP/IP or UDP/IP: This includes any application that accepts these protocols and follows the rules defined in the EMS Developer's Kit.

- `opcmsg` method (for VPO): This option is used for VantagePoint/Operations notifications.

- SNMP traps: This option can be used with any application that accepts SNMP traps, such as NNM or VPO. You need to set up the application to recognize the SNMP traps generated.

- Email: This option does not require any extra handling. Specify the email address when the monitoring request is created.

- Syslog and textlog: This option does not require any extra handling. Specify the log file when the monitoring request is created. Syslog notifications go to the local system.

- Console: This option does not require any extra handling. Specify the console when the monitoring request is created. Notifications go to the local system.

- ServiceGuard: In the case of ServiceGuard, the client application and target application are the same and reside on the same system.

Basic Monitoring on a Single System

A simple monitoring scheme is typically a software program that runs continuously (or at frequent intervals) on a system and tests one or more conditions. For example, a simple monitor could constantly check the number of users logged on to a particular system using the HP-UX `who` command, and when the number of users exceeded a certain level, a message could be displayed.

The following figures show how such a monitor could work. In Figure 4.6, a monitor is running on a system that has only three users logged on. Before the monitor can report an event, at least one more user must log on to the system.

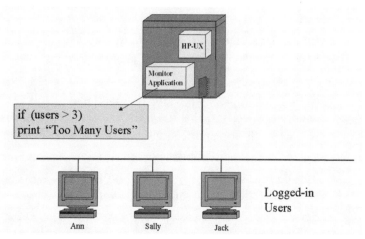

Figure 4.6 *Monitor Testing for Users Logged In*

In Figure 4.7, one additional user has logged on, which results in the monitor's sending out a notification. In the example, the notification appears on a computer screen, but in fact, event notifications can be expressed in any form and can be sent any-where. Instead of a message on a console, a pager notification could be used, or a flashing red icon could be shown on a man-agement display.

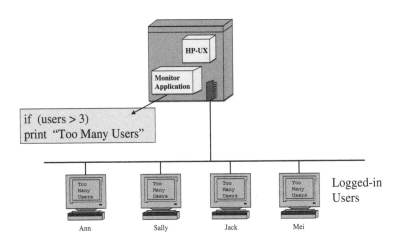

Figure 4.7 Monitor Reporting an Event

Monitoring with Failover

The same type of monitoring could be used in an HA cluster to adjust system load by moving a package from one node to another when the load on the first node exceeds a certain threshhold. Figure 4.8 shows a cluster with a package on Node 1 before the threshold is reached.

Figure 4.9 shows the cluster and package location following an event at which the threshhold was exceeded. In this case, the package has failed over to the second node.

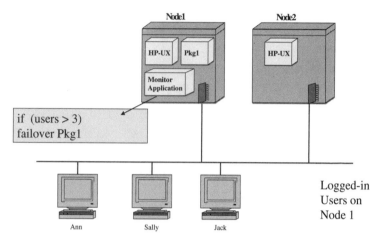

Figure 4.8 *Cluster Before Threshhold*

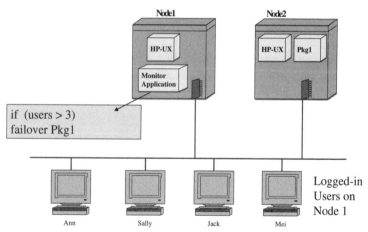

Figure 4.9 *Cluster After Threshhold*

Creating New Monitors

The EMS framework contains an application programming interface (API) along with the registrar and resource dictionary. You can use the API to create customized monitors for use with client and target applications, such as the EMS GUI or Service-Guard. Monitor components to be created include: resource dictionary, resource monitor binary file, man page (recommended), and message catalog (recommended).

Managing Groups of Monitors with EMS

In an HA environment, there are many components that must be monitored constantly to ensure that SPOFs do not develop and persist, leading to an outage. HP's EMS framework provides a common foundation for creating, deploying, and administering monitors of many different kinds. The framework is designed to work in conjunction with standard system management tools such as SAM in HP-UX and OpenView Vantage Point Operations.

Event monitoring techniques allow you to automate the management of systems to a large degree. The outcome of the monitoring activity can be as simple as writing to a log file, or it can be as complex as triggering a package failover or sending an alarm that alerts a system administrator to the circumstances of a failure. Monitoring may be combined with ServiceGuard package configuration, allowing you to define failover following particular events.

Note the distinction between *status* and *event*: an event occurs at a specific moment in time when a predefined criterion (for example, number of logged-in users > 100) is met; status is ongoing, with emphasis on the value for a criterion over a range of time (for example, a file showing the number of logged-in users at each 10-minute interval throughout the day). Monitoring through EMS can be used to track status as well as to report on or react to events.

HA Monitors

High availability monitors are available as separate HP products to provide monitoring of disk resources, network components, and system elements that are tracked in MIB (managed information base) files on the host system. You first create monitoring requests, then start a monitor running. The HA monitors include a disk monitor, a monitor for relational databases, and a set of system and MIB monitors.

The disk monitor monitors LVM disk objects and lets you define monitoring based on logical volume status, number of copies of a logical volume, and a logical volume summary, physical volume status, and physical volume summary. The cluster monitor reports on the status of the cluster, nodes, and packages. The network monitor checks LAN interface status. The system monitor can be set up to track number of users, job queue size, and file system free space. The database monitor obtains information about database servers such as Oracle or Informix.

Hardware Monitors

Many hardware components from HP and from other manufacturers are now available with monitoring software that uses the EMS framework. Here is a partial list:

- Disk arrays
- SCSI tape devices
- HA storage system
- FibreChannel SCSI multiplexer
- FibreChannel adapters
- FibreChannel arbitrated FC switch hub
- Memory
- Kernel resources
- SCSI cards

In addition to the EMS framework, the hardware monitors also utilize the hardware instrumentation that is built into the system hardware and OS. Some monitors also use the logging provided by the support tools manager.

The hardware monitor environment can be complex, involving many layers of instrumentation and logging coupled to the EMS framework. Figure 4.10 shows an example.

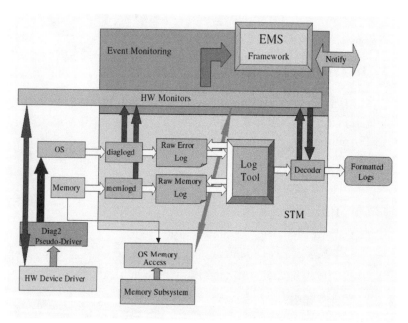

Figure 4.10 *Hardware Monitoring Infrastructure*

Some hardware monitors provide their own configuration clients that handle the EMS configuration as well as the configuration of other components that provide data to the monitors.

ServiceGuard Manager

A new generation of monitoring tools is represented in the Java-based GUI ServiceGuard Manager, which displays cluster maps and shows all the objects in a cluster together. ServiceGuard Manager also lets you save graphical images of clusters and data files containing the details of cluster implementation. A typical ServiceGuard Manager screen is shown in Figure 4.11.

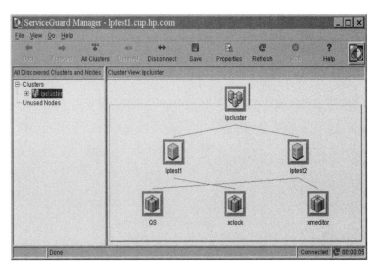

Figure 4.11 *ServiceGuard Manager Screen*

ServiceGuard Manager provides a graphical map that displays all the configured objects in a ServiceGuard cluster and shows all their properties on property sheets. This tool lets you see a cluster's configuration at a glance and determine whether everything is running correctly. Understanding status in this way lets the administrator quickly identify the areas where intervention is needed. A typical cluster map is shown in Figure 4.12. Small badges next to cluster objects indicate problem areas.

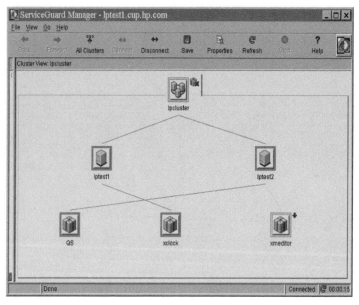

Figure 4.12 *ServiceGuard Manager Map*

This kind of mapping tool with the use of color codes, flags, and so forth is actually a very sophisticated extension of the simple basic monitor described in the beginning of this chapter. The GUI builds an analog for the "flashing light" on the device that indicates failure.

Of course, ServiceGuard Manager is doing far more than that as well. It shows the relationships among the cluster objects, and it allows you to view the properties of particular parts of the cluster. It permits refreshing the display to show the dynamic shifting of states among the cluster objects, and it lets you capture data and graphics in files for later use.

Cluster objects appear in a Windows Explorer-style list at the left in a typical display, Cluster maps appear on the right-hand side of the display. You can capture a graphic image of this map in a file for use in documenting the cluster at any point in its life.

Properties of clusters, nodes, packages, and other objects can be seen through a very complete set of property sheets. An example of the property sheet for a specific package is shown in Figure 4.13.

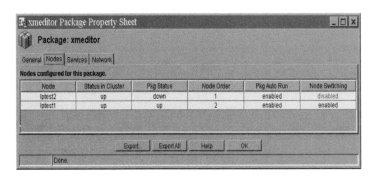

Figure 4.13 *ServiceGuard Manager Package Property Sheet*

Sheets like this can be used to plan changes to the cluster and to observe characteristics of the cluster as it runs. When the state of an object changes—for example, when a package is moved from one node to another—the property sheets show the details as soon as the display is refreshed.

A help system is also provided, as shown in Figure 4.14.

Figure 4.14 *ServiceGuard Manager Help*

ServiceGuard Manager runs on HP-UX and Linux worksta-tions and Windows systems as well as on ServiceGuard cluster nodes. It can run either with a connection to a live cluster or with a cluster representation stored in a file. For example, you can capture a cluster configuration in a file and then display the data on a laptop at a meeting where the ability to connect to the live cluster may not exist.

High Availability Observatory

High Availability Observatory (HAO) is a suite of tools, technologies, and support processes that provides a secure, high-speed infrastructure to support heterogeneous UNIX and Windows NT environments. The basic architecture of HAO includes hardware and software installed at the customer site as well as systems running at the HP Response Center. Components of HAO include:

- On-site support node
- Configuration tracker and analyzer
- HP Predictive
- HA Meter
- HAO Reporter
- Security analysis tools

On-Site Support Node

HAO includes an HP-owned support node that is installed at the customer site to obtain and report on current hardware, software, and network configuration data and change history, and to store system dump files. This node can link to support applications in the mission-critical support center to allow collaboration with support engineers for quick detection of problems and implementation of fixes.

Configuration Tracker and Analyzer

Configuration Tracker automatically tracks hardware, software, and network configuration changes. It also detects patch, service note, and firmware problems in system configuration data, and captures an up-to-date picture of the network topology for the fastest possible problem-resolution times. The Analyzer software at the response center can determine whether the configuration is up-to-date and appropriate, or whether additional patches need to be applied.

HP Predictive

HP Predictive is a toolset that monitors system hardware and reports on current problems. HP Predictive is capable of discovering system behavior that may lead to problems later. This allows you to replace components before outages occur.

HA Meter

HA Meter accurately identifies events that contribute to downtime and automatically calculates the level of availability of systems that support your critical business activities. HA Meter runs as an EMS monitor that tracks the availability of both stand-alone servers and ServiceGuard clusters, nodes, and packages.

Availability data is collected by HA Meter agents running on each monitored system and stored in the on-site repository. Data from the repository is used by HP support personnel to:

- Record information on downtime events.
- Report system availability over time.
- Provide an event history of all downtime occurrences.

HA Meter's ability to provide a consistent and automatic measurement of system availability enables customers and HP's support teams to benchmark various IT process improvements that have been implemented over time and help customers understand where some common causes of downtime can be avoided. Ultimately, this information will help IT departments create more accurate service level objectives for their customers.

HAO Reporter

HAO Reporter is a tool that generates summary information based on configuration and usage data accumulated on the support node. Reports are created on the support analysis system in the response center. Report information includes the following:

- Availability
- Patch summary
- LVM layout
- Disk usage
- Network parameters

Security Analysis Tools

Another component of HAO is called MEDUSA (master environment for detection of UNIX system anomalies). This is a group of programs that help maintain security and auditability.

System and Network Management Products

A number of system and network management products are also particularly relevant to our discussion of HA. The following are described here:

- HP Process Resource Manager (PRM)
- HP-UX Workload Manager (WLM)
- HP ClusterView Network Node Manager (NNM)
- HP NetMetrix
- HP Vantage Point Operations (VPO)
- HP OpenView AdminCenter

HP Process Resource Manager

HP Process Resource Manager (HP PRM) is a tool that lets you allocate specific amounts of CPU, memory, and disk to particular HP-UX processes. The result is that processes achieve the correct balance of resources over time, as shown in Figure 4.15.

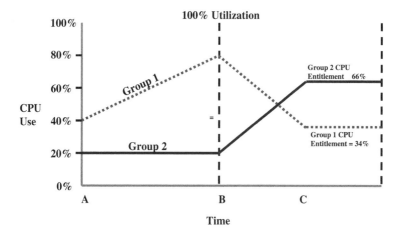

Figure 4.15 *Balance of Resources with HP PRM*

Figure 4.16 shows how HP PRM can be used in an enterprise cluster with MC/ServiceGuard. Before a failure of Node 1, Pkg A has 100% CPU on Node 1, and it is the only package running. Node 2 is running two packages, one with 60% CPU, the other with 40% CPU.

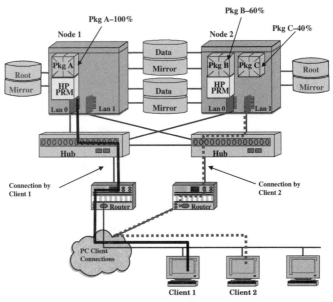

Figure 4.16 *ServiceGuard and PRM: Before Failover*

After a failover, the three packages are given different allocations, as shown in Figure 4.17. These adjustments can be made manually by an operator, or they can be automated inside ServiceGuard package control scripts.

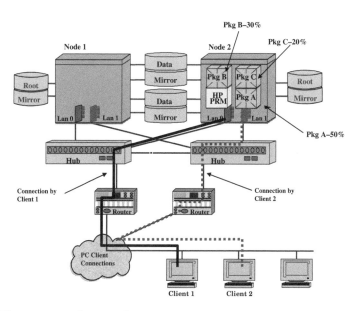

Figure 4.17 *ServiceGuard and PRM: After Failover*

HP Process Resource Manager is tightly integrated with HP's performance analysis tool, HP GlancePlus, allowing HP PRM to be monitored from the graphical interface in GlancePlus. These products combine to both monitor and control the processing environment.

Workload Manager

HP-UX Workload Manager (WLM) provides automatic resource allocation and application performance management through the use of prioritized service level objectives (SLOs). Workload Manager manages workloads as defined in a configuration file. You assign applications and users to workload groups. Workload Manager then manages each workload group's CPU, real memory, and disk bandwidth resources according to the current configuration. If multiple users or applications within a workload group are competing for resources, standard HP-UX resource management determines the resource allocation. Workload Manager builds on the features of PRM, providing a superset of PRM's functionality. Consequently, many of the PRM commands are available within WLM.

Network Node Manager and ClusterView

HP OpenView is a framework for monitoring and administering large networks of systems, including clusters. Network Node Manager (NNM) displays graphical maps of your networks, using icons for each cluster and each node, as well as icons for each package attached to the node on which it currently resides. These icons let you tell at a glance the status of individual cluster nodes. For those nodes that are running packages, ClusterView lets you monitor the state of each node and package by observing its icon. When failovers occur, the icons representing nodes and packages change color to alert the operator of the change. During a failover, the package icon can be seen to move over to an alternate node. As an example of ClusterView's interface, a detailed view of the nodes in a group of clusters is shown in Figure 4.18.

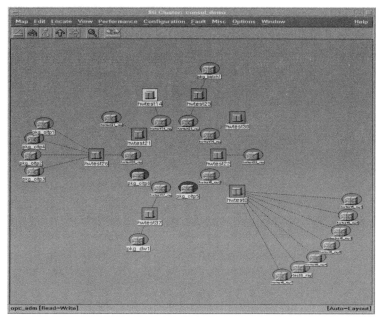

Figure 4.18 *ClusterView Detail of Clusters and Nodes*

ClusterView is expected to be replaced by ServiceGuard Manager, which was described earlier in this chapter.

HP NetMetrix

HP NetMetrix is a distributed internetwork monitoring and analysis system that proactively monitors the network and allows you to configure the network optimally, providing instant remote network access for rapid problem resolution. HP NetMetrix allows you to baseline critical information such as network utilization, broadcast packets, error rates, and any other parameters deemed critical. HP NetMetrix measures statistics over a long period to yield a true operating envelope. After baselines are established, events that fall outside the envelope can be detected and reported as early warnings of network problems.

HP NetMetrix can be valuable in tracing the patterns of network traffic in a complex network such as a network used in HA clusters.

Vantage Point

HP OpenView Vantage Point is a system management tool that automates and centralizes the management of multi-vendor distributed systems. It monitors systems on the network and then reports and responds to various system alerts throughout the distributed environment. (This is in contrast to network alerts, which are handled by NNM.)

Vantage Point also allows operators to use a GUI to carry out scripted recovery actions needed in response to various cluster, node, and network events. The expertise and knowledge of more experienced operators can be captured and used for the benefit of more junior operators. This guided action speeds the recovery process. As an alternative, Vantage Point provides smart plug-ins (SPIs), which are agents that automatically respond to an event, notifying the operator of action taken.

Another feature of Vantage Point is the ability to shift management control and information flow among multiple management centers. A large company, for example, might have major management centers in New York and Los Angeles sharing responsibility for system management. Using Vantage Point's Operations Center, they could shift control automatically from one coast to the other in a process known as "follow the sun" management.

OpenView AdminCenter

Another OpenView product that helps improve the availability of distributed environments is AdminCenter. This is a systems management tool that automates the configuration change process for distributed systems. It assists administrators in planning and executing configuration changes to software, file systems, peripherals, system configuration, and kernels from a central location.

AdminCenter also helps reduce operator errors by substantially reducing complexity. A good example of this is the "universal add" concept. With HP-UX, adding a new user might involve a number of different actions: creating the user, login, home directory, etc. Creating each of these different objects typically requires the operator to memorize completely different commands for adding the various objects. Instead, AdminCenter substantially reduces complexity by allowing the operator to automatically add a user by selecting a single icon. AdminCenter automatically performs all the actions needed to add all of the objects for the new user.

Another HA feature of AdminCenter is the ability to simulate proposed changes. AdminCenter will display the predicted results of proposed changes in a graphical form, allowing the operator to analyze the proposed changes and to correct mistakes *before* doing the actual implementation. This helps eliminate mistakes and associated downtime.

Finally, AdminCenter also helps manage the software environment by providing the ability to distribute software. This applies to multiple vendor platforms and includes the ability to both pull and push software updates. This feature can substantially reduce the complexity of coordinating software revisions, thereby saving time.

Memory Monitoring and Deallocation

A final addition to the HA product family is a facility called dynamic memory page deallocation. This is a background diagnostic that periodically inspects the memory logs for single-bit memory errors. It then proceeds to inspect the specific bytes of memory that contained these errors to determine whether a hard error (a permanent single-bit error) exists. If a hard error exists or if the error is a repeating single-bit error, the 4K block of memory that contains the error will be dynamically removed from the OS's allocation tables.

This diagnostic improves availability by preventing hard single-bit and repeating single-bit memory errors from turning into double-bit memory errors (which will halt systems).

ServiceControl Manager

Today's HA clusters are increasingly complex, with a large number of nodes and a growing array of hardware components. To avoid the problem of complexity leading to unwanted downtime, it is essential to choose system management tools that simplify and streamline the routine tasks needed to keep the cluster running smoothly. This applies to all system management tasks, from the creation of accounts through the definition of networked file systems. But for clusters, it is essential to carry out the following multi-node tasks carefully:

- Installing software
- Managing the cluster configuration
- Managing security

HP's ServiceControl Manager (SCM) provides an environment that can simplify these processes. Using SCM, you create a central management server that contains a repository of the software and configuration settings required for your environment. Then, using distributed management tools, you can quickly set up a group of systems with identical software versions, appropriate kernel configurations, similar cluster software configurations, and security arrangements. Figure 4.19 shows a high-level view of this approach.

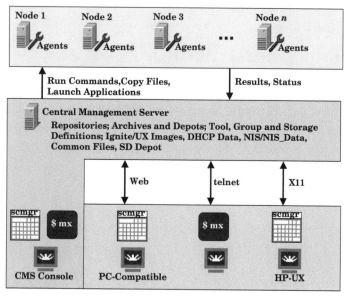

Figure 4.19 *ServiceControl Central Management*

SCM Tools

ServiceControl Manager is the GUI that coordinates the activities of defining the software content and configuration of groups of systems and taking the steps necessary to automate the creation of groups of correctly configured systems. The Tools screen from this interface is shown in Figure 4.20. The following sections describe some of these tools in a little more detail.

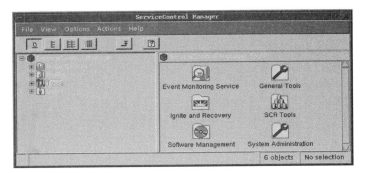

Figure 4.20 *ServiceControl Tools Screen*

Event Monitoring Service

Event monitoring is the configuration of monitors across groups of nodes. As shown earlier in this chapter, monitors provide early detection of faults that can result in loss of availability. This section of ServiceControl lets you configure monitors across groups of cluster nodes rather than individually on each node. Where large groups of systems are involved, setting up monitors can be time-consuming without special tools like the EMS.

Ignite and Recovery

This area in ServiceControl lets you define the content of a system very precisely and then implement the definition on particular nodes using HP's Ignite-UX software. You can also restore systems to a known baseline or recover systems whose software has become non-functional or misconfigured. This area also lets you capture and store baseline images of software that can be implemented on other systems. Some of these functions are shown in Figure 4.21.

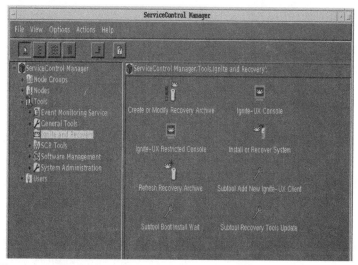

Figure 4.21 *SCM Ignite and Recovery Tools*

Software Management

ServiceControl Manager also provides a set of software management tools that can be used on multiple systems. The essential functionality is provided by Software Distributor. Through SCM, you can create Software Distributor depots from which the installation of multiple systems can be staged. After installing software once on the central management station, you can then install to a large group of nodes in the most efficient manner. Some of these operations are shown in Figure 4.22.

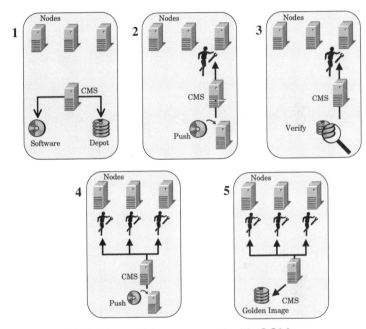

Figure 4.22 *Software Management with SCM*

CHAPTER 5
Disaster-Tolerant High Availability Systems

*H*igh availability clusters can provide protection against SPOFs for your applications and services running on clustered HP systems. But there are many events that can cause *multiple* outages in a system, either simultaneously or in quick succession. Furthermore, though these events sometimes affect only a single system, they can frequently have a dramatic impact on an entire data center.

How do you protect your application and its data from acts of violence like the bombing of the World Trade Center in New York? From violent weather conditions such as the hurricanes and tornadoes that have recently affected Europe and North America? From earthquakes around the Pacific rim? From acts of war? What can you do to keep a disaster from making the company's entire IT operations unavailable?

Most of the solutions described so far in this book have been implemented on a single site, with a group of up to 16 clustered systems located in an individual data center. **Disaster-tolerant solutions** actually extend the scope of HA from the level of the hosts in an individual data center to the level of alternate data centers on the same site, alternate sites in a large metropolitan area, or over distances of hundreds or thousands of miles. They do this by placing cluster nodes in locations that are remote from each other, or by creating backup clusters that can run mission-critical applications in the event of disaster. In this way, the cluster itself can be eliminated as a point of failure.

This chapter discusses various kinds of disaster tolerance that you can obtain through extensions to the basic cluster technology presented earlier in this book. The topics include:

- Types of Disasters
- Disaster Recovery Planning
- Disaster-Tolerant vs. Highly Available
- Protecting Data from Disaster
- Disaster-Tolerant Architectures
- Local Clusters
- Campus Clusters
- Metropolitan Clusters
- Continental Clusters
- Business Recovery Services

Types of Disasters

High availability solutions are designed to cope with individual failures within a system or cluster of systems. A disaster, however, may involve multiple failures, or it may result in cascading failures over wide geographic areas. A **disaster** is usually defined as a set of extreme circumstances resulting in dramatic, catastrophic loss to a large number of people (Figure 5.1). A disaster frequently involves great economic loss and sometimes entails significant loss of life.

Figure 5.1 Disaster!

Protection of the essential services provided by a business is especially important during and after a disaster, not only because the business loses money when it is unable to provide goods and services, but because the affected communities in a disaster may need those services to recover. For example, insurance providers, financial service organizations, medical care facilities, and public utilities must all be ready to carry on as quickly as possible.

Case in Point...

The costs of disaster can be astronomical—in human as well as financial terms. The loss of a business is not just a financial burden on the company that is hit by the disaster, but on all those who depend on its services, employment, and tax contributions. The *Disaster Recovery Journal* (Summer 1999) reviewed the effects of tornadoes that hit Oklahoma and Kansas in May of 1999:

> In total, 742 people were injured and 41 people died from the storms, with five deaths occurring in Kansas. Damage estimates in Oklahoma show 2,314 homes were destroyed; 7,428 homes were damaged; 1,041 apartments were destroyed or damaged; 164 businesses destroyed; and 96 businesses were damaged.... According to preliminary figures from Insurance Services Office, Inc's (ISO) Property Claim Services (PCS) Unit, Oklahoma received a record catastrophic loss of $955 million for insured property. Property losses in Kansas totalled $100 million.

Disaster Recovery Planning

Many large companies and institutions develop and maintain disaster recovery plans to assist in coping with the aftermath of a hurricane, earthquake, flood, or other large-scale catastrophe. Needless to say, a good disaster recovery plan requires management buy-in at the highest levels in the organization. Planning can fail when managers do not understand what constitutes a critical business activity and what is dispensible.

The first step is defining what you understand a disaster to be. For example, how do you define a minor disaster, a major disaster, and a catastrophic disaster? One possible set of definitions appears in Table 5.1. Criteria like those described in the table can be used in deciding when to go into a disaster recovery mode, that is, when to take recovery action.

Planning is documented in a **disaster recovery plan.** This is a written document that details the steps to be taken by each department. A comprehensive plan will include plans for staffing each operation when it is being run at a different location, sometimes far distant from the original site. The disaster recovery plan for the overall business includes payroll and benefits management, customer service and support, on-line services provided to customers and employees, and general communication services such as telephone and network systems. It also includes employee safety, assessment of damages, and estimated repair times.

Table 5.1 *Disaster Criteria*

	Minor	Major	Catastrophic
Duration of Outage	1 day	1 week	> 1 week
Hardware Damage	20% of servers damaged	50% of servers damaged	> 50% of servers damaged
Network Losses	1 subnet of 4 down for more than 1 day	All subnets down for more than 1 day	All subnets down for more than 3 days
Data Loss	Lost transactions that were in progress	Lost previous 24 hours of data	Lost more than 24 hours of data
Software Condition	Able to run critical applications with reduced efficiency	1 business-critical application down for more than 2 days	More than 1 business-critical application down
Data Center Facilities	Some power loss	Loss of protection for applications	More than 50% power loss

Following are some of the most important components of the business recovery plan:

- Employee safety and awareness
- Emergency response
- Relocation of critical business units
- Public relations and media response

Data Center Recovery Plan

For IT organizations, the disaster recovery plan will deal with matters such as the restoration of data from tapes to backup systems and the deployment of computer systems at alternate sites. It will include separate sections for batch operations, for on-line transaction processing (OLTP), and for client/server operations such as the company Web servers and Intranet servers for use by company employees.

Table 5.2 highlights some of the most important components of the business recovery plan. Disaster planning is frequently done in conjunction with consulting organizations that help assess an organization's susceptibilities to different disasters, write the plan, and then rehearse its features with staff members.

Table 5.2 *Data Center Recovery Plan*

Areas	Plan will include...
Site and Facilities Recovery	Deployment of maintenance crews to inspect and document damage and estimate repair time and cost
Computer Recovery	Replacement of broken host systems
Work Area Recovery	Cleanup of minimal required environment or move to an alternate site
Telecommunications Recovery	Develop site plan in conjunction with phone company for complete testing of phone systems
Network Recovery	Test each subnet; replace broken cables, hubs, router systems, or set up new subnets
PC Recovery	Replace broken systems or deploy PCs at an alternate site
Data Recovery	Restore data from backups; deploy systems at alternate sites
Application Recovery	Move applications to alternate systems or alternate sites

Clustering Solutions as Part of Disaster Recovery

High availability clusters can make many important contributions to a complete disaster recovery solution. While no single technology or product is likely to be able to address every circumstance, many of the disaster-tolerant clustering solutions described in this book can be incorporated into a comprehensive disaster recovery plan. For example, the disaster-tolerant metro-cluster and continental cluster architectures described in the next sections can be major components in the disaster recovery plan for a data center.

Disaster-Tolerant vs. Highly Available

Disaster tolerance is the ability of a system to survive a disaster. In most cases, this means the ability to endure **multiple points of failure** (MPOFs). In the extreme case, this can include the loss of an entire data center and all its functions. Not all HA components and systems can be considered disaster-tolerant.

How can you make an HA cluster disaster-tolerant? The answer depends on the degree of tolerance to multiple failures you want to achieve. This in turn has financial consequences, because the most fault-resilient systems are also the most expensive.

Different degrees of protection can be provided for your IT infrastructure. Each level of protection has its own requirements and associated costs and benefits. In ascending order of cost and complexity, Table 5.3 outlines several possible levels of protection you can establish using HA cluster technology.

Table 5.3 *Types of Protection Through Clusters*

Type of Protection	Clustering Strategy	Cost
Protecting data	MirrorDisk/UX, RAID with disk arrays, backup technology	$
Protecting the network	Redundant hubs, switches, and routers to keep users connected and maintain connections between systems	$
Protecting the application	Redundant applications through HA clusters; multiple instances of an application on different systems	$$
Protecting individual hardware units and clusters	Increasing the distance between the nodes of a cluster and between the mirrors of the disk storage media	$$$
Protecting a company site	Providing still greater distances and completely separate data storage facilities on different sites	$$$$
Protecting a regional operation	Replicated clusters across long geographic distances	$$$$$

The protection of company sites and regional operations requires a disaster-tolerant architecture that goes beyond the capabilities of the single cluster described so far.

What Is a Disaster-Tolerant Architecture?

In an MC/ServiceGuard cluster configuration, HA is achieved by using redundant hardware to eliminate SPOFs. This protects the cluster against hardware faults such as the node failure depicted in Figure 5.2. This example shows a local cluster in which a package that was running on Node 1 runs on Node 2 following the failure. In most cases, this example would be implemented in a cluster with a group of nodes located in the same data center, often the same building, and frequently the same room.

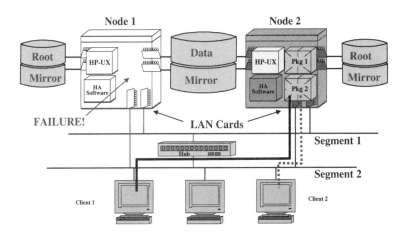

Figure 5.2 *Failover in a Local Cluster*

For some installations, this level of protection is insufficient. Consider the order processing center where power outages are common during harsh weather, or consider the systems running the stock market, where multiple system failures, for any reason, have a significant financial impact. For these types of installations, and many more like them, it is important to guard not only against SPOFs, but against MPOFs, or against single massive failures that cause many components to fail, as in the failure of a data center, an entire site, or a small geographic area. A **data center**, in the context of disaster recovery, is a physically proximate collection of nodes and disks, usually all in one room.

Creating clusters that are resistant to MPOFs or single massive failures requires a different type of cluster architecture called a **disaster-tolerant architecture**. This architecture provides you with the ability to fail over automatically to another part of the cluster or manually to a different cluster after certain disasters. Specifically, the disaster-tolerant cluster provides appropriate failover in the case where a disaster causes an entire data center to fail. In Figure 5.3, we see a cluster in which the nodes are spread between two data centers that are physically separated from one another. The packages use mirrored disks, with each disk mirrored by a separate physical volume in the other data center.

Following a fire at Data Center A (Figure 5.4), packages are able to start up on the nodes in Data Center B, which is not affected by the fire.

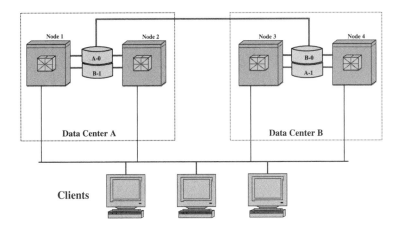

Figure 5.3 *Disaster-Tolerant Architecture with Two Data Centers*

Protecting Data from Disaster

All disaster recovery solutions, like all HA solutions, must incorporate an approach to data protection. As shown in Chapter 2, eliminating SPOFs in the disks in a cluster is the first start. A backup strategy is also essential, so that recovery is possible from stored backup data when everything else is lost. Backup solutions have the disadvantage, however, of being very slow. It can take a long time to restore a large database and then reapply transaction

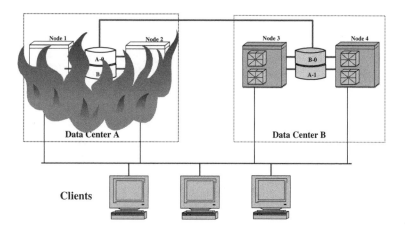

Figure 5.4 *Failover Between Data Centers*

log files. And of course, data is lost since the last backup. Other types of data replication offer protection and less loss of data and time.

Mirroring and some of the RAID modes are actually simple forms of data replication that occur within a single disk array or between individual disks that are in very close physical proximity to the node that is reading or writing data. For longer distances, data must be transmitted over high-speed links between disk devices that are geographically dispersed. Such solutions are slower, because of the distances involved, and more expensive, because of the need for high-speed leased lines.

Data replication can be done by means of products that employ dedicated special hardware, or by means of software solutions. Two examples of the former are the HP SureStore Disk Array XP series and the EMC Symmetrix. An example of the latter is the Oracle Standby Database.

Physical Data Replication

Physical data replication is the writing of the same stream of bits to more than one location to provide an exact copy of the data that is placed on a storage medium. Physical replication includes copying everything that is processed between an application and the disk, including temporary data that is backed out, or transactions that are never completed.

Physical Data Replication Using the XP Series

The HP SureStore Disk Array XP series allows you to carry out physical data replication by setting up a link between two separate arrays and setting up primary volumes (PVOLs) on one array that correspond to secondary volumes (SVOLs) on another array. The two arrays can be separated by large geographic distances, which can be cross-continental, if wide area networking is used. Figure 5.5 shows how this looks.

Physical Data Replication Using the EMC Symmetrix

Physical data replication on the EMC Symmetrix is done in a similar way, with volumes on the primary disk array known as R1 volumes and volumes on the remote disk array known as R2 volumes.

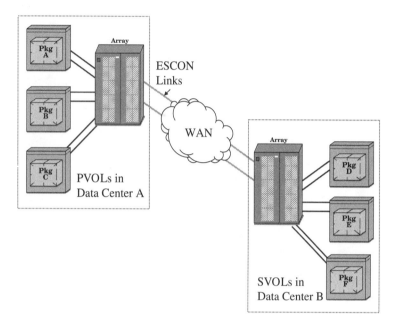

Figure 5.5 *Physical Data Replication: XP Series*

Logical Data Replication

In logical data replication, the aim is the same as with physical replication—to provide a duplicate copy of data that can be used in another location in the event of disaster. But with logical replication, the emphasis is on replicating the transaction rather than the physical I/O operation. This can be done by copying log files from one data center to another and applying them to an alternate database. This is the method used by the Oracle Standby Database product. (Note that this type of replication works without a large disk array.)

The process is shown in Figure 5.6.

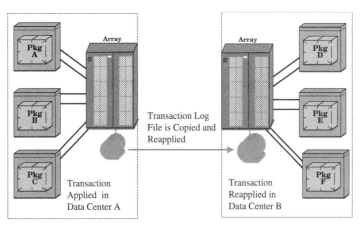

Figure 5.6 Logical Data Replication

Protecting Networks and Storage Links

It is also important to eliminate points of failure in network and data storage links so that they will function appropriately during and after disaster events. Many kinds of redundancy can be provided for these links, and examples are shown elsewhere in this book. These include:

- Redundant subnets
- Backup hubs and switches that are cabled to all host systems

- Redundant routers
- Duplicate long-distance fiber optic cabling
- Duplicate Gigabit Ethernet cabling

Whatever your choice of network or data storage link technology, you must provide protection of the cable from potential breakage, as in what has come to be called the **backhoe problem**. In this classic situation, an outage occurs when a construction worker, during excavation on the site, accidentally severs the main communications link with a backhoe (see Figure 5.7).

Figure 5.7 *The Backhoe Problem*

On your own property, you can control this problem by routing redundant cables through different trenches dug on different parts of the property. This would prevent the destruction of one cable from bringing down your entire operation. In WANs, you can obtain redundancy by using different lines at the phone company, provided you can determine that the different lines actually use different physical cables. Since phone companies frequently lease one another's lines, you have to make sure you do not inadvertently route the redundant lines through the same physical cable, which then becomes an SPOF (see Figure 5.8).

Figure 5.8 *The Backhoe Problem Avoided*

Disaster-Tolerant Architectures

The remainder of this chapter describes a number of cluster solutions that can be useful in creating a disaster recovery plan. Differing amounts of disaster tolerance are provided by the following cluster architectures:

- Local clusters
- Campus clusters
- Metropolitan clusters
- Continental clusters

The greater the separation between components of the cluster, the higher the degree of disaster tolerance. The next few sections show how these cluster types provide disaster tolerance.

Local Clusters

A local cluster has all nodes located in a single data center. Because most HA clusters are local clusters, this type is included in the discussion as a baseline for comparison with other cluster architectures.

Local clusters generally do not provide disaster tolerance because their components are all located in relatively close physical proximity. In the event of an earthquake, for example, rack-mounted systems in the same computer room may actually roll into one another; in the case of a fire, the high temperature in the room affects all components in essentially the same way—all of them experience essentially the same physical effects of the catastrophe. However, the local ServiceGuard cluster is the start for a comprehensive disaster-tolerant solution, because a disaster-tolerant solution should be highly available too.

A local cluster is shown in Figure 5.9. All the components are assumed to reside within a single data center, Data Center A.

Campus Clusters

An additional degree of protection is afforded by moving cluster nodes further apart. **Campus clusters** are ordinary MC/ServiceGuard clusters in which the nodes are distributed as

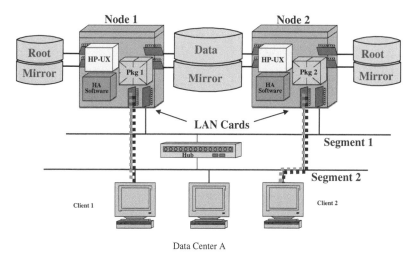

Data Center A

Figure 5.9 *Local Cluster*

widely as possible within the property lines of the organization. There is no need to provide leased lines or private communications links. The nodes in a campus cluster are connected according to specific guidelines for disaster tolerance using high-speed cables.

A **campus cluster** has alternate nodes located in different data centers. These data centers can be separate rooms in a building, adjacent buildings, or even buildings separated by some distance. In a campus cluster, it is assumed that the owner of the cluster has exclusive control of the land and buildings of a multibuilding corporate site. The word "campus" implies that the organization housing the cluster owns or leases the land and buildings such that no outside permission is needed to dig trenches, lay cable, or reroute power circuits. This makes it possible to provide redundant power circuits, and it allows you to provide separate, redundant data communication lines on different parts of the site. Campus clusters are designed so that no single building failure will cause the cluster to fail.

Campus clusters are connected using a high-speed cable that guarantees network and data access between the nodes as long as all guidelines for disaster-tolerant architecture are followed. The distance between nodes in a campus cluster is limited by the data replication technology.

Architecture requirements for campus clusters usually consist of:

- Redundant disks using data replication. An example of this is HP's MirrorDisk/UX, which replicates data to two disks of any type. Physical volume links (PV links) are used to provide redundant physical paths to the data.
- Redundant network cables installed using different routes. This protects the cluster from a single accident severing both network cables at once.
- Power for each data center supplied from different power circuits. Some may even want to lease redundant power from different substations. This protects the cluster from a single power failure due to shorts or accidents that cut power to all nodes in the cluster.

- A campus cluster with four nodes must use dual cluster locks to provide a tie-breaker in case the heartbeat is lost among the nodes. As an alternative, the campus cluster can use arbitrators if it follows the same rules as the metropolitan cluster designs (see Figure 5.12). However, the conventional four-node campus cluster uses dual lock disks.

Campus clusters are implemented using standard MC/ServiceGuard with FibreChannel mass storage.

An example of a campus cluster appears in Figure 5.10.

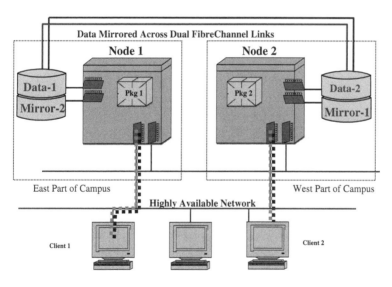

Figure 5.10 Campus Cluster

When there is a failure in the campus cluster environment, the architecture can provide a far higher degree of protection for the systems than the local cluster alone. Of course, the campus cluster provides all of the protections of the local cluster; but also, it protects against events that destroy or disable an entire physical location, such as the building that houses a data center. If there is a major fire in a data center, an entire cluster could easily be destroyed. By using the campus cluster model, another building across campus can provide the necessary redundancy to keep applications available to clients. This is shown in Figure 5.11.

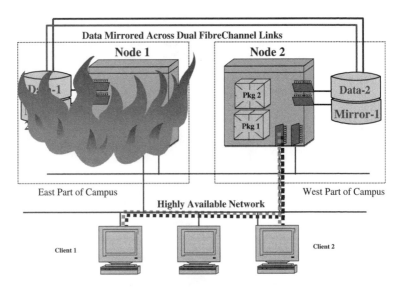

Figure 5.11 Campus Cluster After Failover

Metropolitan Clusters

As the name suggestions, a **metropolitan cluster** operates within a metropolitan area; nodes may be separated by geographic distances no greater than 43 kilometers (25.8 miles). A metropolitan cluster operates much like an ordinary Service-Guard cluster, with some additions:

- Special disk array hardware and software for data replication are used.
- Special control scripts are employed for packages.
- Arbitrator systems are used as tie-breakers instead of lock disks.

A metropolitan cluster has nodes located in different parts of a city or in adjacent cities. Putting nodes further apart increases the likelihood that alternate nodes will be available for failover in the event of a disaster. However, there is a tradeoff: Increasing the distance also increases the expense of the cluster and the complexity of the environment.

Metropolitan clusters are very similar to campus clusters with the exception that metropolitan clusters often require rights-of-way from local governments or utilities to lay network and data replication cable. This can complicate the design and implementation. Metropolitan clusters also require a different kind of tie-breaker system for ensuring that split-brain situations do not arise. Typically, metropolitan clusters use an arbitrator site containing additional cluster nodes instead of cluster lock disks. Metropolitan cluster architecture is shown in Figure 5.12.

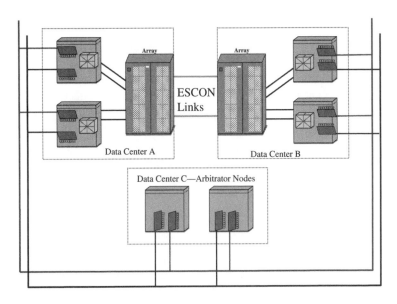

Figure 5.12 *Metropolitan Cluster Architecture*

The architectural requirements are the same as for a campus cluster, with the additional constraint of the third data center. And as with a campus cluster, the distance separating the nodes in a metropolitan cluster is limited by the data replication and network technology available. Metropolitan cluster architecture is implemented through two HP products:

- MetroCluster with Continuous Access XP

- MetroCluster with EMC SRDF

A key difference between campus and metropolitan clusters is the data replication technology used. Campus clusters use FibreChannel and MirrorDisk/UX, which limit the distance between data centers to a maximum of 10 km (6 miles). Metropolitan clusters use data replication based on the capabilities of the HP SureStore Disk Array or the EMC Symmetrix array, which allow greater distances—up to 43 km (25.8 miles).

What happens in a disaster? Suppose an explosion destroys Data Center A in the example shown in Figure 5.12. The result is given in Figure 5.13—operations continue at Data Center B.

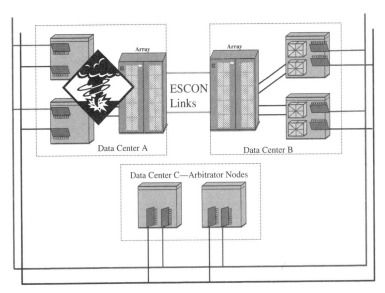

Figure 5.13 Metropolitan Cluster After Failover

Continental Clusters

A **continental cluster** provides alternate *clusters* that are separated by large distances connected via wide area networking. This allows you to configure clusters that back each other up over wide geographic distances and permits a failover from one cluster to another. All protected applications are started in the new location when a determination is made that the primary cluster is no longer available.

The design is implemented with two distinct ServiceGuard clusters located in different geographic areas. In this architecture, each cluster maintains its own quorum, so an arbitrator data center is not used. Continental clusters are architected to use any WAN connection via TCP/IP protocol; however, due to data replication needs, high-speed connections such as T1 or T3/E3 leased lines or switched lines may be required. Continental cluster architecture is shown in Figure 5.14.

The key issues concerning a WAN cluster are:

- Inter-cluster connections for continental clusters are TCP/IP-based connections.
- The physical connection is one or more leased lines managed by a common carrier. Common carriers cannot guarantee the same reliability that a dedicated physical cable can. The distance can introduce a time lag for data replication, which creates an issue with data currency. This could increase the cost by requiring higher speed WAN

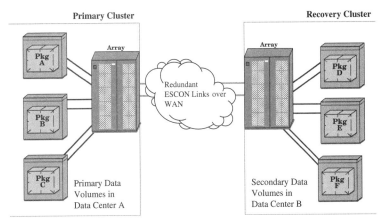

Figure 5.14 *Continental Cluster Architecture*

connections to improve data replication performance and reduce latency.

- Tools such as TP monitors or database replication tools that work across a WAN are needed to make sure the replication maintains data consistency.

- Operational issues, such as working with different staff with different processes and conducting failover rehearsals, are made more difficult as the distances between the nodes in the cluster increase.

Figure 5.15 shows a continental cluster operating normally with applications running on the West Coast and systems available on the East Coast for quick failover.

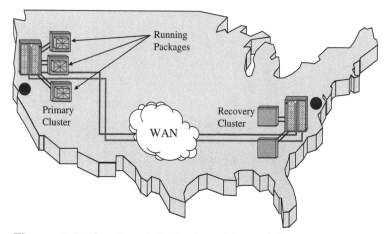

Figure 5.15 *Continental Cluster—Normal Operations*

The aftermath of a disaster on the West Coast is shown in Figure 5.16.

Continental clusters are implemented using HP Continental Clusters. This product is used in conjunction with ServiceGuard clusters that are set up in two or more separate geographic regions such that one cluster backs up another. This solution uses physical data replication provided by HP's XP Disk Array series or by the EMC Symmetrix, together with high-speed long-distance links and ESCON converters. As an alternative, it is possible to use logical data replication via software products such as the Oracle Standby Database and similar products from other vendors.

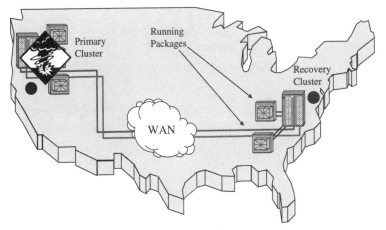

Figure 5.16 *Continental Cluster Failover*

Extensions to Continental Clusters

Extensions of the basic continental cluster architecture might include the following:

- Two data centers backing each other up in a bi-directional configuration
- One recovery data center backing up several primary data centers
- Metropolitan clusters backed up by a recovery cluster in another geographic region

Examples are shown in Figure 5.17 and Figure 5.18.

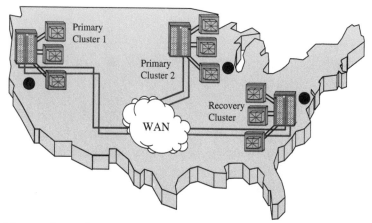

Figure 5.17 *Continental Cluster with Two Primary Clusters*

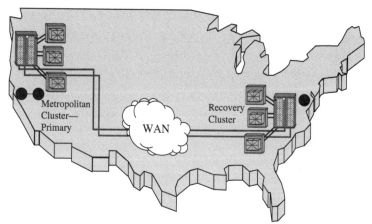

Figure 5.18 *Continental Cluster with a Metropolitan Cluster as the Primary Cluster*

A Note about Costs

The configurations shown in this chapter represent fairly expensive solutions compared with the cost of stand-alone systems or simple clusters created with MC/ServiceGuard. The deployment of redundant HP 9000 systems and disk arrays, the use of multiple separate data centers, the added requirement of specialized data replication software, and the lease of cables for data and network transmission will create significant capital and operating expenses. However, the cost needs to be weighed against the type and degree of risk to the enterprise. As with other kinds of HA, disaster-tolerant solutions provide a significant level of insurance for the corporation's mission-critical operations.

One way of containing the cost of disaster recovery is to out-source the disaster-tolerant configuration. It is possible to contract for services that will provide the capabilities needed following a disaster. Off-site facilities can be leased at remote locations; often, these can be prepared for a quick transition to everyday business routines within a few hours to a few days. HP itself provides leased backup facilities in several locations across the U.S.

Business Recovery Services

Business recovery services help companies maintain or recover their critical IT-based business processes following natural disasters, man-made disasters, and critical hardware/software failures. Examples of critical business processes include a just-in-time inventory system, the call center of a telephone company or electric utility, or even a corporate general ledger.

The term "business recovery" is used instead of "disaster recovery" when the focus is on the recovery of entire business processes rather than just the recovery of computer systems and network infrastructure. The term "business continuity" is often used as a synonym for "business recovery," although most properly, "business continuity" is an even broader term that covers all technology, people, and processes intended to ensure the continuity of a company's business processes.

Business recovery may require the deployment of staff and infrastructure in unusual ways following a calamity. People may have to report to a different physical site, sometimes at a great distance from the original site, and continue performing their tasks in an unfamiliar environment. Frequently, a smaller crew is required to perform a subset of the tasks that are done during normal operation. Systems such as mail delivery, shipping, and receiving are often handled in less efficient ways. Providers of services such as telephone and networking are required to re-route communications. Business recovery thus is far more than simply bringing the computer system back on-line: it means bringing an entire organization back to an acceptable level of function as quickly as possible.

How Are Business Recovery Services Delivered?

Business recovery delivery is usually provided through a shared subscription service that allows subscribers access, in the event of a disaster, to a fully functional alternate computer facility or to a computer system shipped to a location of their choice. For highly mission-critical environments, business recovery may be accomplished with fully redundant dedicated systems and storage. Business recovery delivery services also include the provision of alternate office facilities, complete with desks, PCs, and call center equipment.

Business recovery consulting complements the delivery services by providing a full range of consulting services, including business impact analyses (BIAs), disaster mitigation analyses, and business recovery plans.

HP's Recovery Service Products

HP offers a full spectrum of business recovery services to fit the value and recovery needs of each of your business processes. These services are differentiated primarily by the recovery time objective (RTO)—the length of time between disaster declaration and the point at which your end-users can reconnect to their important business applications. The services also differ in their recovery point objective (RPO)—the timeliness of the data being automatically restored as part of the recovery process.

With all of these services, except BRS Basic, highly trained and experienced recovery specialists assist customers during both disaster rehearsals and actual disasters to help ensure a smooth recovery. In particular, rehearsals are considered to be consultative learning experiences for our customers and a key part of HP's offering. Several types of HP services are shown in Figure 5.19.

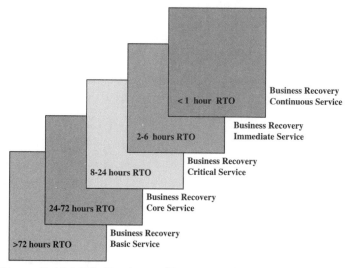

Figure 5.19 HP's Business Recovery Service Types

CHAPTER 6
Enterprise-Wide High Availability Solutions

*H*igh availability clusters let you eliminate points of failure in most of the components that run a sophisticated application. But some of today's enterprise-wide IT solutions employ multi-tiered applications and clusters, which must be kept available as well. Solutions discussed in this chapter are as follows:

- Storage Area Networks
- Shared Tape Solutions and HA Omniback
- Highly Available SAP
- Consolidating Applications in HA Clusters
- 5nines:5minutes

Storage Area Networks

A storage area network (SAN) is a group of centralized storage resources that can be accessed via high-speed, high-bandwidth links and that can be managed together. A SAN is different from storage that is directly attached to a particular host (usually via SCSI) and from storage that is attached through ordinary networks, as in NFS-mounted file systems. A SAN attempts to provide the performance of direct-attached disks and the flexibility of attaching large amounts of storage to multiple hosts. The most advanced features in a SAN increase server performance, optimize storage use, assist in load balancing, provide management capability, and enhance HA.

A SAN that is composed of disk arrays using RAID configurations and redundant links together with highly available management software can enhance the availability of data and application services throughout the enterprise. SANs can be designed to work smoothly with heterogeneous groupings of servers and disk hardware, including HA clusters.

A SAN offers many benefits for the enterprise:

- Redundant paths to data: There can be several paths to data from the servers to the storage device.
- Performance: The primary LAN is not affected because data access is over a dedicated network.

- Centralized management: Backups can be carried out from the perspective of enterprise data instead of one host at a time.

High-Speed FibreChannel Interconnect

Storage area networks are made possible by high-speed interconnects on high-capacity communications fabrics such as FibreChannel. Using the older SCSI bus technology, access to disk data for reading and writing was limited by the length of the SCSI bus itself, which required connected units to be physically close to one another. With Fast/Wide SCSI architecture, the maximum distance between units (server to disk or server to server) is about 25 meters (81 feet).

The key to success in developing a SAN is the ability to interconnect a variety of devices and to add and remove storage within the network in a flexible manner that responds to the need for growth and easy maintenance of the disk inventory. Ideally, SANs provide any-to-any communication between hosts and storage resources, including host servers and storage devices. The network is built using FibreChannel switches, hubs, and bridges, which are crucial components in the SAN. Typical SAN components are shown in Figure 6.1. An example of a SAN configuration operating alongside a ServiceGuard cluster is shown in Chapter 7.

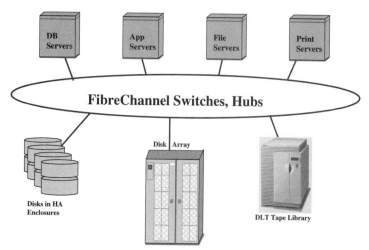

Figure 6.1 *Storage Area Network*

FibreChannel—the fabric that enables SANs—is an ANSI-defined high-speed protocol. With a speed of up to a Gigabit per second currently, it uses large, variable-length block sizes for data transfer between systems and peripherals of different types. Both networking and mass storage are supported (though most vendors do not currently support networking), as well as transfer to print and tape devices. FibreChannel protocol is supported over both copper and optical cables. FibreChannel allows distances of up to 10 km (6 miles).

Tools for SAN Management

To provide ease of management when configuring SAN storage and for monitoring and managing data, HP provides two software tools:

- SAN Manager Device Manager (DM)
- SAN Manager LUN Manager (LM)

Managing Physical Devices with SAN Manager DM

HP SureStore E SAN Manager DM manages devices in the SAN in the same way that OpenView NNM manages devices on a TCP/IP network. The scope of SAN Manager DM is all the physical devices that comprise the SAN installation. This includes not only the servers and disk systems, but also the FibreChannel switches, hubs, and bridges that interconnect the segments of the SAN. All components must be configured to function together smoothly.

SAN Manager DM provides a centralized management console from which the enterprise can manage the FibreChannel infrastructure and all the storage devices attached to it. Devices can be added, deleted, or changed from a single interface, which is composed of device maps. Disk devices and servers from a variety of different vendors can be displayed, together with their FibreChannel interconnections, including redundant connections between devices. SAN Manager DM auto-discovers devices that are part of the SAN topology, including server-based FibreChannel host adapters, storage devices, and interconnecting devices, such as hubs, switches, and bridges.

Devices are mapped in an intuitive graphical format at a central console, which gives the IT operator an instant view of the SAN in all its aspects. Continual automatic discovery ensures that changes in the SAN are quickly identified and mapped.

Devices can be configured and monitored from SAN Manager DM. This is especially useful for the FibreChannel interconnect devices so that the enterprise can regulate access to all components and ensure that faults are detected quickly. The console can be used to launch device-specific management interfaces; more than one application can be associated with each device, and applications can be Web-based or server-based.

A software developer's kit (SDK) is also available to permit integration of new devices into the DM framework.

The basic SAN Manager DM device map display is shown in Figure 6.2.

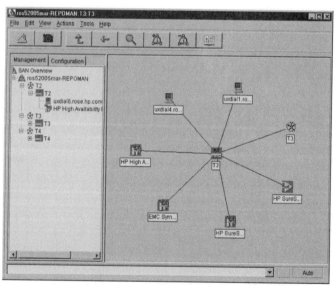

Figure 6.2 SAN Manager DM Device Map Display

Right-clicking on an icon in the device map (for example, an FC30 disk array) lets you display properties of the device represented by that icon, as illustrated in Figure 6.3.

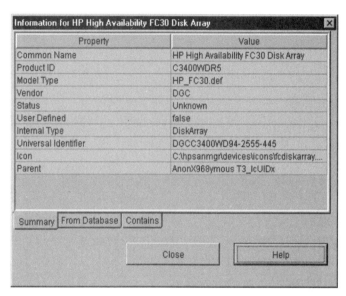

Figure 6.3 SAN Manager DM Device Properties

Another useful screen is the Event Display, which shows entries for events—failures, changes in availability, etc.—that are taking place throughout the SAN. This is shown in Figure 6.4.

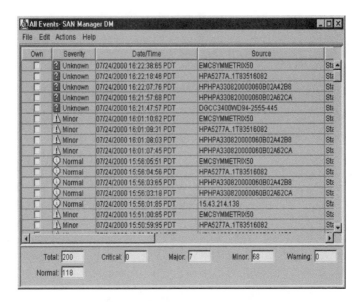

Figure 6.4 SAN Manager DM Event Display

Managing Units of Storage with SAN Manager LM

A SAN is not simply physical devices cabled together, it is also a logical grouping of logical storage units (usually called LUNs) that contain file systems, raw partitions, or other elements that comprise the enterprise data store. A logical view of the data in a SAN is needed to give the enterprise control over its most important resource, information.

Managing access to storage, maintaining it and parcelling it out to users can be expensive and time-consuming. A simple example is the server that has run out of storage capacity. Before

SANs, the IT manager had to bring down the server to add storage capacity; but with the SAN, the LUN administrator can use the SAN admininstration console to view available LUNs and assign one to the server without bringing it down.

Creating a Network Storage Pool

With SAN Manager LM, you create a networked system for administrative clustering that allows LUNs to be securely assigned to designated server nodes on the SAN. The assignments are made dynamically, so that changes can occur without host disruption. A good network storage pool should have the following characteristics:

- Single system image: The network administrator is able to see and manage all nodes and storage subsystems from one console.

- Heterogeneous environment: Servers of different types (including Windows NT and UNIX operating systems) are supported, and different types of HA configurations are supported.

- Cluster support: The SAN's storage units should be capable of simple configuration within clusters for shared storage.

- Granular asset assignment: Storage devices are seen by the SAN on the LUN level, and LUNs can be assigned and reassigned to provide efficient allocation of storage assets.

SAN Manager LM offers these features. Currently, up to 16,000 LUNs and up to 200 server nodes can be managed on a SAN.

Highly Available Storage Database

The SAN Manager LM software has no SPOFs, and therefore its use will not compromise availability. The SAN configuration database can be mirrored up to three ways to ensure that a copy will always be available. Each host accesses the database independently, eliminating run-time interdependencies between hosts. Since hosts are independent, no communication takes place over the messaging network (LAN) unless the IT manager is reconfiguring the SAN. Hence, a host can boot and access all of its assigned storage even if it has temporarily lost its LAN connection.

Console Operation

Using the SAN Manager LM console, the IT manager can view and manage an entire SAN from a central location. The console incorporates a GUI with drag-and-drop capability to make storage assignment fast and accurate. Storage assigned exclusively to each host is clearly displayed in a simple tree structure. SAN Manager LM also provides a way to visualize and manage storage configurations where more than one host must access the same devices. This makes the system especially useful for clustered and shared tape environments.

Most SAN administration tasks are done in SAN Manager LM's main window, which is shown in Figure 6.5.

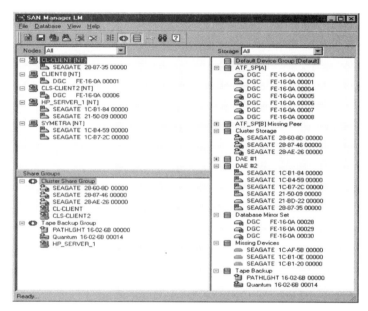

Figure 6.5 *SAN Manager LM Main Window*

The "Nodes" and "Storage" panes are always displayed. For detailed information about a specific storage object in the SAN, you can double-click to drill down and display a screen of additional information, as shown in Figure 6.6.

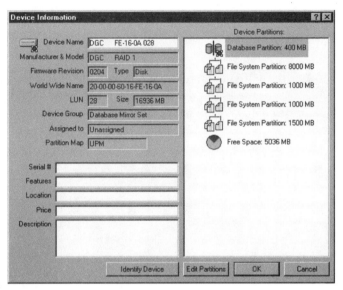

Figure 6.6 *SAN Manager LM Details on a Storage Unit*

Shared Tape Solutions and HA Omniback

ServiceGuard's Advanced Tape Services (ATS) extends the capability of the cluster to include highly available shared tape devices and tape library robotic devices that can be connected to more than one node in the cluster. Shared tape devices can be used for backups of files activated on more than one cluster node. This means that even after a package fails over to another node, a backup of the package data continues or restarts on the alternate node. In combination with backup technologies such as Open-View Omniback, ATS provides a complete HA tape backup solution.

You can configure shared tape devices only between any two nodes in a cluster. While any tape device can be configured for shared use in the cluster, the greatest benefit is obtained with high-end devices such as the HP DLT 4/48 tape library, which has four separate tape drives and a robotic device (a mechanical arm) that loads and unloads up to 48 8GB cartridges.

ATS Features

ATS generates new device files with the same cluster-wide unique name on all nodes that are connected to any shared tape device. This includes tape library robotic devices and individual tape devices. With unique cluster-wide device names for each shared device, applications can use the same device filename for a particular device. This way, the device name is the same no matter what node the application is on.

ATS provides automatic reclaiming, that is, it makes shared devices available to applications on other cluster nodes automatically after a system failure of the node that owns an ATS-shared device.

ATS provides exclusive allocation and access between devices. Only one process on any one host has access to a particular device file at any particular time.

ATS Configuration Types

ATS allows many kinds of configurations, including:

- One magnetic tape device shared between the nodes of a two-node cluster.
- One tape library with four tape devices shared between the nodes of a two-node cluster.
- One magnetic tape device and one tape library with four tape devices shared among the nodes of a four-node cluster.
- Four tape libraries with four tape devices, each shared among the nodes of a four-node cluster.

An HP DLT 4/48 tape library being shared in a two-node cluster is shown in Figure 6.7.

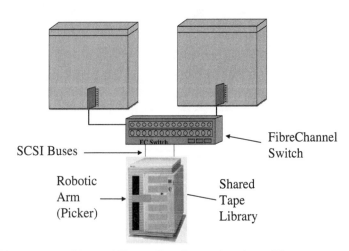

Figure 6.7 *Shared Tape Configuration in a Cluster*

ATS and Omniback

HP Omniback is a part of the OpenView product family that lets you manage a backup strategy across an entire enterprise. Omniback can be configured to operate within the cluster framework, providing backups for data that may be accessed by different nodes in the cluster at different times.

To use ATS devices in the Omniback environment, you simply identify the tape device within Omniback by the cluster-wide unique identifier. Omniback will then route the backup operation to the node that currently has ownership of the device. The backup operation itself, running as a ServiceGuard package, can fail over from one node to another and the backup can continue.

Figure 6.8 shows an HA configuration in which Omniback provides the backup services for an enterprise cluster. This example shows a pair of disk arrays connected to each other with ESCON links. Business copy volumes (BCs) are used as a way of splitting off a unit of storage for backup.

Running Omniback as an HA Package

Omniback runs as a group of separate processes that can be executed on different servers. Backup sessions are checkpointed; after each specific unit of data is backed up, the software marks the backup list to indicate how far it has gone. If the backup is interrupted at any point, it can be continued from the point of interruption at a later time. If all servers are connected to the same data that is to be backed up (via NFS, for example), the backup can recover and then continue on any node without having to start

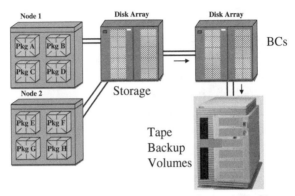

Figure 6.8 *Omniback Configuration in an HA Cluster*

from the beginning. Backup processes can be built into Service-Guard packages so that they can fail over from one server to another. If the process fails over to another node, the checkpointing means that the process can continue on the other node from the beginning of the specified backup that was interrupted when the failover occurred.

Figure 6.9 shows a configuration with ATS and Omniback running in a cluster as a ServiceGuard package. The cluster after failover is shown in Figure 6.10.

Omniback and SAN Configurations

Omniback plays a very significant role in SAN configurations, which are described in more detail earlier in this chapter. By its nature, the SAN requires backup components that are efficient and flexible. Omniback in a ServiceGuard environment also provides the necessary degree of HA for the SAN.

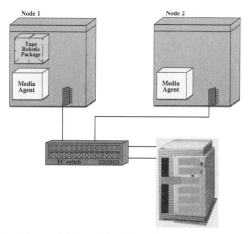

Figure 6.9 *Shared Tape Backup Running as a Package*

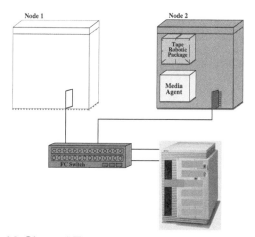

Figure 6.10 *Shared Tape Backup Package After Failover*

Highly Available SAP

SAP software provides the ability to monitor and run all parts of an enterprise, and many businesses are connecting SAP environments to the Internet to create e-commerce applications. In many of these environments, HA is a must. Several of the components of the SAP architecture can be protected by using clustering with the ServiceGuard Extension for SAP. This toolkit integrates MC/ServiceGuard with R/3.

One- or Two-Package Approach

The ServiceGuard Extension for SAP can be implemented in several ways. Typically, the configuration is set up with one or two ServiceGuard packages. In the one-package approach, both the central instance (CI) and the database (DB) run on a single server configured in a single package (A). In the event of failure (B), both move from the primary server to the adoptive server. This approach is illustrated in Figure 6.11.

The most common two-package approach separates the DB and CI into different packages, which can fail over separately to the adoptive server. This is shown in Figure 6.12.

Protecting the Enqueue Service

A significant SPOF in standard SAP R/3 is the Enqueue Service. This component is a part of the CI, and can be configured to fail over in the typical ServiceGuard manner. However,

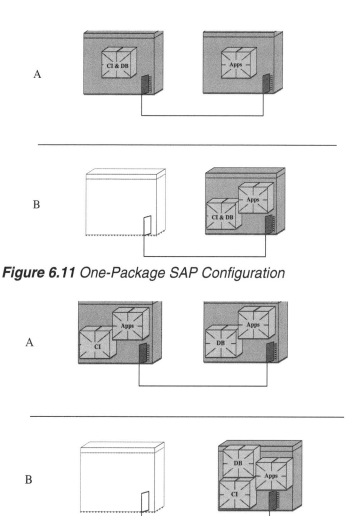

Figure 6.11 *One-Package SAP Configuration*

Figure 6.12 *Two-Package SAP Configuration*

when this failover occurs, all pending user transactions are lost and must be re-entered. This loss of pending transactions can be avoided by using an optional product known as Somersault. HP worked with SAP to develop this technology, which mirrors the Enqueue Service, keeping a copy of the relevant data in an alternative location. Without mirroring, the CI is an SPOF, as shown in Figure 6.13.

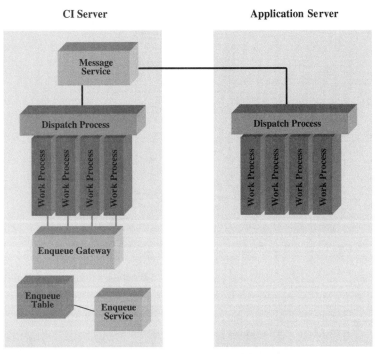

CI Server   **Application Server**

Figure 6.13 Central Instance without Mirroring

HP Somersault technology provides a mirror of the critical elements needed to allow a faster recovery of the CI. In the event of failure, the CI package moves to an alternate node, and the Enqueue Service is recovered from the surviving Enqueue Service mirror. Failover time is reduced significantly compared with the failover provided by the standard ServiceGuard SAP toolkit, and transactions that were queued up prior to the failure do not need to be reapplied. Figure 6.14 shows the mirroring of the Enqueue Service by Somersault.

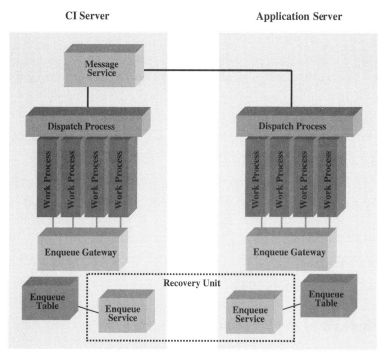

Figure 6.14 Mirroring of Enqueue Service

Consolidating Applications in HA Clusters

HP's first clustering solutions provided HA within the somewhat narrow scope of an individual cluster of HP 9000 systems. Together with highly reliable hardware components, this groundwork provided the means of keeping individual applications and services running. Within this type of cluster, the most common usage model was one server to one application.

Today, a newer generation of more powerful servers allows clusters to run multiple packages with different applications in them, or to run multiple instances of the same package. Advanced HP 9000 architecture allows the partitioning of the host system so that applications can be totally isolated from one another, and failover is possible among multiple partitions of the same system. Clustering technology has also evolved to the point where replicated packages can be run on groups of nodes within a cluster.

Moreover, clustering is available on multiple platforms, and many vendors, including HP, are developing multi-platform solutions that employ Linux and Windows NT/2000, as well as the standard UNIX platform.

The line between availability and scalability is blurring as the Internet comes to dominate more and more enterprise activity. In many Internet applications, availability depends on the capacity to process large numbers of transactions, and this often demands a two-fold strategy for availability:

- Multiple systems hosting replicated instances of the same Web server process
- A highly available database that can fail from one node to another when necessary

An example of this environment is shown in Figure 6.15.

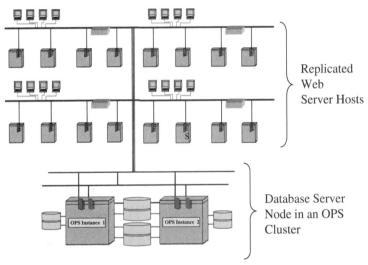

Figure 6.15 *HA Internet Using Both Replication and Failover Technologies*

There is also an increased recognition that HA does not end with the server farm or the individual cluster of nodes; the network is also frequently a point of failure that must be protected by supplying redundant cards, cables, hubs and switches, and routers. And as expansion of on-line storage continues, the SAN must provide HA as well.

Finally, clustering technology must accomodate the needs of users who wish to consolidate multiple applications on larger servers. When it first appeared, clustering drew many applications away from the mainframe environment with the promise of less expense and simpler management resulting from the use of distributed client/server systems. Paradoxically, however, the proliferation of clustering has created a new need for consolidation, and the emergence of more powerful server systems now allows great flexibility in creating consolidation solutions.

Types of Consolidation

Five major types of consolidation are common in the enterprise:

- System management consolidation: Refers to a common system management framework applied across a data center or across an enterprise, as opposed to managing individual systems independently.

- Mass storage consolidation: Refers to the sharing of mass storage devices across a large number of servers, as opposed to a storage device per server architecture.

- Network consolidation: Refers to the sharing of a high-bandwidth interconnect to handle traffic from multiple networks, as opposed to having multiple independent networks.

- Backup consolidation: Refers to the sharing of large-capacity tape backup libraries or silos, as opposed to having a backup device per server architecture.
- System consolidation: Refers to the sharing of systems by multiple applications, as opposed to having a dedicated system per application architecture.

The last of these is the most common candidate for implementation with HA clusters, though the other types may also benefit from clustering. An example of system consolidation is shown in Figure 6.16.

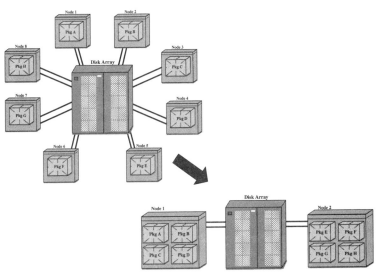

Figure 6.16 *System Consolidation Using Clusters*

5nines:5minutes

5nines:5minutes is the vision of an enterprise HA solution that achieves 99.999% availability, which translates to no more than five minutes of downtime per year. This vision was articulated by HP in 1998 as a goal for the development of HA solutions by the HP R&D community and their partners by the end of the year 2000. The architecture for 5nines:5minutes involves custom-designed components provided by HP and numerous partners in the computer industry—including BEA, Cisco Systems, Oracle Corporation, and EMC Symmetrix.

This section outlines a solution that provides much of the infrastructure required to achieve this vision. 5nines:5minutes has been a considerable challenge, because it is clear that the many components of the total solution—including components from different vendors—must all work cooperatively to produce the desired outcome.

> *NOTE:* 5nines:5minutes is a complex software and hardware solution that requires a very significant consulting and support effort to implement. This section is an attempt to give only a broad sketch of the technology

Solution Requirements

As an enterprise-level transaction processing solution, 5nines:5minutes requires a robust database environment together with a transaction monitor to route transactions to the correct destinations, and a set of applications to perform database access operations.

To obtain information about the operating environment, the OpenView Vantage Point Service Navigator was tailored to include a number of smart plug-ins (SPIs), which provide data from running systems to the management workstations running on a separate cluster equipped with Service Navigator tools.

Special requirements for data replication include the ability to write data to two different disk arrays separated from each other by a physical firewall, and also to mirror the data to another set of disk arrays at a remote site. Local and remote data replication use different technologies—the local replication is done synchronously, while the remote mirrors are created with asynchronous writes that preserve the ordering of I/O operations.

To demonstrate that HA levels have been achieved, special monitoring tools are needed to record all instances of downtime and provide an audit trail of all incidents of outage and return of service. In addition, special support services and change management processes must be used to ensure that outages are handled as quickly and efficiently as possible. With a level of availability stretched to 99.999%, monitoring has been extended to encompass nearly every corner of the solution hardware and software.

5nines:5minutes Architecture

The 5nines:5minutes solution was designed as a high-end system for enterprises that need disaster tolerance across great geographic distances as well as very high levels of availability. The initial system uses monitoring with Vantage Point Operations Center, the OpenView system management solution. It also employs an Oracle database and TUXEDO transaction monitoring in redundant configurations. The solution developed for the first release also includes a wide-area disaster-tolerant component like that of ContinentalClusters (but using a different technology). Figure 6.17 shows the basic architecture.

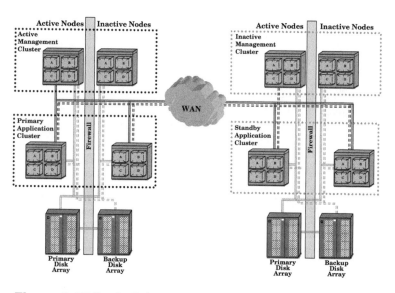

Figure 6.17 Basic 5nines:5minutes Architecture

In this design, two data centers are separated by a significant geographic distance linked by WAN technology. Within each data center, applications run on clustered servers using ServiceGuard OPS Edition. The nodes of each cluster are separately powered, and physically separated from each other by a literal firewall. Each node is connected to a pair of high-capacity XP series disk arrays, which are used in a Continuous Access configuration to back each other up.

Data Redundancy and Replication

Transactions are applied on the local site to the database, which is built using OPS. A standby instance of OPS, also on the local site, is ready to come into use as soon as a problem is detected in the main instance. The database is replicated to the remote site using Oracle's Standby Database product. In the event of a switch to the remote site, OPS instances will start up on the remote site, and the standby database will switch into use with an OPS instance. A complex set of scripts and special tools ensure that the remote and local sites are coordinated, and that data is acessed on only one site at a time.

In addition to the protections implemented at each separate data center, data is mirrored over the WAN from one site to the other. Thus, double-failover protection is provided: local and long-distance switches are possible for either planned or unplanned failover.

Monitoring and management software are also included in redundant forms on both sites. This software is designed so that management operations can easily shift from one site to the other in a "follow the clock" system management model. The design also emphasizes flexibility—many functions can be automated, or they can be carried out by operators using commands.

Use of Clusters

Four clusters are used in this design: two at the primary site and two at the remote site. One cluster handles the main database and its applications. This cluster uses packages and other special tools that are responsible for:

- Starting and stopping OPS database instances
- Launching the transaction monitor, BEA TUXEDO
- Managing the archive log files created by Oracle
- Creating business copies (BCs) on the XP series disk arrays
- Logging and managing error conditions that arise in 5nines:5minutes components

The second cluster is known as the management cluster. It does the following:

- Runs Vantage Point (formerly called OpenView IT/Operations), including the Service Navigator component, which displays every monitored service within the entire 5nines:5minutes environment

- Runs the Event Analyzer, which can trigger an automatic local or global failover when necessary

The management cluster also runs its own Oracle database, which contains Vantage Point data.

Local Control

Local Control is responsible for launching various services on the front-end processor. Local Control is actually a Service-Guard package that can fail over to another cluster node within the local data center. The Local Control package starts up a variety of services, some of which are run as separate packages. For example, the OPS instance on one node in the primary cluster is started as an active instance, and the OPS instance on the other node in the primary cluster is started up as an inactive instance, which serves as a standby that is ready to quickly switch to the active role to accept transactions if the current active instance fails.

Another important service that is started by the Local Control package is the TUXEDO gateway process, which is used to direct client database transactions to the appropriate server. Under normal circumstances, the gateway will send transactions to the active OPS instance currently running in the cluster. In addition to the gateway, the Local Control package also starts up TUXEDO server processes on both nodes.

In addition to the OPS instances, the Local Control package starts up an archive file manager, which recycles OPS log files, and a BC manager, which controls the creation of BCs that can be used for backups.

Also running in the front-end processor under the control of the Local Control package are the Vantage Point agents (also known as smart plug-ins, or SPIs). These agents continuously monitor the condition of the important software and hardware components and report incidents (events) to the Vantage Point software that runs on the management cluster.

Most of the services described here are configured as ServiceGuard packages, but the configuration is different from that of conventional packages in several ways. For example, packages in 5nines:5minutes are node-specific, that is, they do not automatically fail over to the other node under ServiceGuard's control. Instead, the Local Control package starts up the services described here by using the `cmrunpkg` command and shuts them down using the `cmhaltpkg` command. This lets 5nines:5minutes avoid the relatively slow process of failover and bring up the service very quickly in an alternate location. There is no need for package failover because the backup packages are already up and running on other nodes.

The behavior of the Local Control package is shown in a simplified form in Figure 6.18.

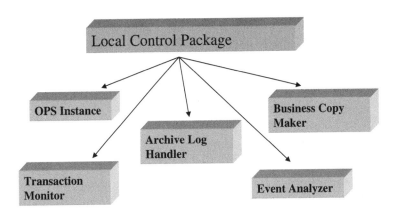

Figure 6.18 *Local Control Operations*

Global Control

Global Control, running on the management cluster, handles situations in which it is necessary to switch from one data center site to another. This software resides in a package that runs on the management servers of both sites.

Global failover can be automated, or it can be carried out by a series of special-purpose commands that are provided as part of the 5nines:5minutes software.

Global failover in 5nines:5minutes uses a different technique for providing long-distance cluster recovery than that used in ContinentalClusters (described in Chapter 5). The monitoring requirements of the 5nines:5minutes environment are so different, and so demanding, that a new approach had to be created.

Data Replication Techniques

As with other kinds of HA solutions, ensuring that there are redundant copies of data is essential. The 5nines:5minutes software uses three kinds of data replication:

- Synchronous physical data replication between the disk array frames at each site.
- Asynchronous replication of the log files, which are then applied to the remote database, which is configured with the Oracle Standby Database product.
- Business copy volumes created by the disk array software. Business copies can be used for creating tape backups at either site. In the event of complete data loss at one site, the BCs created on either site could serve as the source of a restored database.

Monitoring and Management Approach

Nearly every component in the 5nines:5minutes environment is monitored using EMS monitors (described in Chapter 4) or special Vantage Point SPIs, which are designed to send messages to the Vantage Point console for operator action. Special

SPIs are used to monitor OPS, TUXEDO, the 5nines:5minutes core software components, disk array hardware, and other components as well.

The tool used for monitoring on a service-by-service basis is the Vantage Point Service Navigator. Many of the monitored services are displayed on the management workstation, together with status information. Specific events are chosen to trigger automatic operations such as a local failover. Other events (disk failure, for example) require operator intervention (replacing the physical disk module), and these are flagged with messages telling the administrator what action to take. Service Navigator, which is a part of the OpenView product suite, displays each service and lets you observe the details.

From the Vantage Point workstation, you can take action directly on particular nodes, or you can issue Local Control or Global Control commands to do such things as fail over locally, fail over globally, start or halt individual components, view log files, and do other system administration tasks. If an automated action is already in progress, this action takes precedence over operator commands. A typical Service Navigator screen is shown in Figure 6.19.

Local Database Failover

A failover from one node to another in the local cluster may take place for several reasons:

- Node-specific failure on the local site
- Routine maintenance required on one node

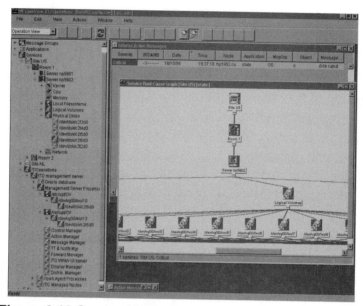

Figure 6.19 *Service Navigator Display*

- Application error on one node

During a local failover, a variety of processes, configured as ServiceGuard packages, switch over to the alternate node at the local site. After the problem has been identified and fixed, or when node maintenance is complete, the application can be returned (failed back) to the original node, if desired. A special 5nines:5minutes command is used to do this failback.

The failover and failback described above are similar to the standard ServiceGuard failover and failback, with a few additions:

234

- Failover of several packages takes place at once, and in a particular sequence.
- Failover is based on monitoring that is done by SPIs and EMS monitors, not ServiceGuard alone.
- The database instance does not actually fail over from one node to another; transactions are simply directed to the other instance on the alternate node by the TP monitor as a part of the local failover process.

Global Database Failover

If something happens to the entire local site, such as a natural disaster, the operation will fail over globally to the remote site, where the database will switch from a standby database to a set of OPS instances. This failover, which takes more time than a local failover, results in the remote cluster assuming the complete personality that was formerly held by the local cluster.

Following a global failover, the local cluster can be converted into the remote role, in which case Oracle Standby Database is enabled, and the formerly remote site becomes the primary site. Alternatively, the database can be made to fail back to its original home.

Management Operation Failover

The services running in the management cluster can also fail over from one node to another locally, or they can be switched globally "with the clock" to allow the management function to be carried out in daytime hours across the globe. In this case, the main database is still located at the primary site, but the monitoring of the Service Navigator display can be done in different places at different times for convenience.

Software Configuration Management

An important part of the 5nines:5minutes vision is the management of a mission-critical configuration over time. This requires establishing clear documentation of the initial state of the configuration, then tracking every change that takes place. Changes need to be tested carefully on development environments before being rolled into the 5nines:5minutes production system. A large part of the consulting that accompanies a 5nines:5minutes implementation involves setting up change management processes that allow users to perform normal upgrades, carry out needed modifications, and apply required patches with minimal impact on the availability of the system. Such processes allow the vision of 99.999% availability to remain essentially unchanged, even as business needs evolve.

CHAPTER 7
Sample High Availability Solutions

*H*igh availability clusters provide a sturdy foundation for supporting mission-critical applications. For optimal availability, clusters and the processing environment they support should be designed from top to bottom for HA; the cluster should be constructed in a way that eliminates any SPOF. System management tools should be deployed, and environmental factors such as power failures should be addressed.

This chapter presents a few examples of HA configurations that solve real business problems:

- Highly Available NFS System for Publishing
- Stock Quotation Service
- Order Entry and Catalog Application
- Insurance Company Database
- Disaster-Tolerant Metropolitan Cluster for City Services

- SAN Configuration for an Internet Service Provider

These hypothetical examples are suggestive of ways you can use HA clusters and subsystems for your mission-critical applications. Note that all the examples are considerably simplified.

Highly Available NFS System for Publishing

A large publishing company has chosen to use an HA cluster to support document production. This system uses highly available network file services (NFS). NFS is a general facility for accessing file systems remotely over a LAN. In the example that follows, the NFS server software is made highly available so that writers and editors do not lose access to their NFS-mounted file systems for an extended period if the NFS server should fail. Figure 7.1 shows the basic configuration for this active/standby MC/ServiceGuard cluster.

High Availability Software and Packages

The HA software coordinating the activities of the cluster is MC/ServiceGuard, which runs on both nodes in the cluster. The NFS server processes run as a package on one node in the cluster. Initially, the package runs on the primary node, shown on the left in Figure 7.1. The package configuration file identifies the nodes

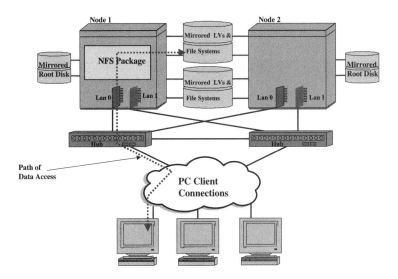

Figure 7.1 Highly Available NFS Server System

on which the NFS server processes can start up at different times and specifies which node is the primary node for NFS services. A separate package control script contains specific commands for starting up and halting the NFS services. This control script is installed on both nodes in the cluster.

Copies of the NFS server software must exist on both nodes in the cluster—in this case, on each node's root disk. An NFS package template is available as an MC/ServiceGuard toolkit to help in setting up this configuration. The template contains sample configuration files and control scripts, which you can customize as needed.

> *NOTE:* Even though one node in the configuration serves as a standby for the NFS package, that node may also be used for different packages or for applications that are not configured as packages.

Hardware Configuration

One possible hardware configuration for a highly available NFS server is described in the following sections.

Two SPUs

The configuration shown in Figure 7.1 shows two HP 9000 Series L-Class SPUs. This setup provides the capacity for a large number of clients to access NFS mounted data.

Mirrored Disks and JFS File Systems

Disk mirroring is controlled by HP's MirrorDisk/UX, and file systems are configured with HP's Journaled File System, or JFS (bundled with HP-UX). The configuration uses individual mirrored disks holding the file systems that will be exported for NFS mounting by external clients. The use of individual mirrored disks provides good performance while ensuring that data is not lost in the event of a disk failure. Each mirror copy is connected to both cluster nodes by means of a separate disk controller. Mirroring is therefore done between disks that are on separate buses.

In addition, disks are installed in enclosures that permit hot-plug replacement of disk modules while the system is running.

Redundant LAN Hardware

Figure 7.1 shows an Ethernet configuration in which one LAN card on each node is active and the other is on standby. The active LAN carries file server requests from clients and also the cluster's own heartbeat messages.

Responses to Failures

Some of the most common failures are the following:

- Disk failure
- Disk controller failure
- LAN adapter failure
- LAN cable failure
- SPU or OS failure
- NFS software failure

How does this NFS server cluster react to some of these possible situations?

Reaction to Disk Failure

If there is a failure in one of the pair of mirrored disks, the cluster will continue to use the copy of data on the other disk. The failed disk must then be replaced. This means installing a new disk, then allowing the disks to re-synchronize via MirrorDisk/UX. The client will not notice any loss of service.

If the failure is in a controller card, the cluster will continue to use the mirror copy of data, but the failed controller card must be replaced during a period of scheduled maintenance. This requires bringing down the cluster. Detection of the failure is through the HA disk monitor, which searches for particular error states and reports events via EMS, the Event Monitoring Service. Operations Center (OpC) can also be used for this monitoring.

Reaction to LAN Failures: Local Switching

If a LAN card fails, MC/ServiceGuard automatically switches to the backup card and continues processing. If the problem is transitory, then the other card remains available for local switching. If the card has had a hardware failure, then it must be replaced, which requires removing the node from the cluster, powering it down, and replacing the defective hardware. On power-up, the node will rejoin the cluster and the new card will become the primary LAN card.

Figure 7.2 shows the effect of local switching. If something happens to the current LAN, MC/ServiceGuard will switch to a standby interface, and the path of access to the NFS-mounted file system will be preserved.

Reaction to LAN Failures: Remote (Package) Switching

If there is no standby LAN card available, the package running on Node 1 will restart on Node 2, and clients may experience a brief loss of service during the package switch.

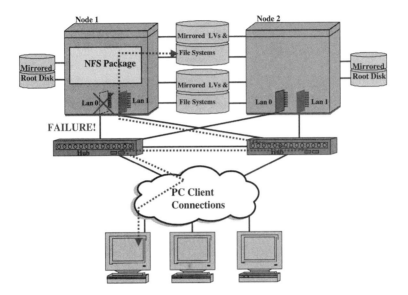

Figure 7.2 *NFS System After Local LAN Switching*

Figure 7.3 shows the cluster's state following a remote switch, that is, a switch of the package from one node to the other.

In this case, there is a delay as the NFS server processes start up on the backup node, activating and exporting the file system that is to be NFS-mounted from elsewhere.

Note that even with a package switch, the client does not need to reconnect. For example, suppose a writer is in the middle of updating a chapter. Just after a "save" command is issued, the node fails. In this case, the "save" will hang until the NFS server

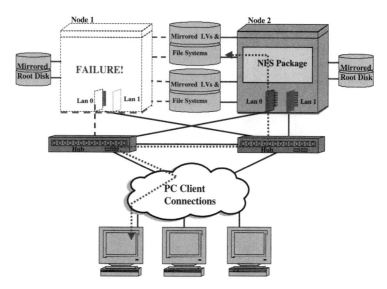

Figure 7.3 *NFS System After Remote (Package) Switching*

comes up again on the alternate node, then the "save" will complete. During this process, the writer will experience an outage of about one minute.

Reaction to SPU or OS Failure

If the SPU experiences a failure, or if the OS experiences a panic (fatal error), the node will shut down and MC/Service-Guard on the other node will start the package in its alternate location. The failover should take about 30 seconds in addition to the time required to start NFS.

Reaction to NFS Software Failure

MC/ServiceGuard monitors the health of the NFS processes. If a failure occurs, the package containing all NFS services and file systems fails over to the other node in the cluster. The failover should take about 30 seconds in addition to the time required to start NFS.

Stock Quotation Service

The following is an example of an application that uses an MC/ServiceGuard package to provide highly available stock quotation and analysis services.

A brokerage firm, Baxter On-line Investment Services (BOIS), provides a stock quotation service to its clients, who can log on from networks or home computers and obtain a quotation on the stocks in their portfolios. The quotations are provided from a price table that BOIS obtains from the stock exchange computer system.

Each quotation nets BOIS about $2.25 in fees. The average volume of queries nationwide is 500 per minute, for a total amount of $1125 per minute, or $67,500 per hour. Though not all of this would be lost in an hour of downtime, a considerable fraction would not be recovered through later queries. There is another potential loss of income as well. Since BOIS is also a full-service investment broker, clients frequently monitor the market themselves and call to order a transaction based on what they see. Thus, the loss of the quotation service would also result in the loss of brokers' commissions.

High Availability Software and Packages

BOIS stock services use three related applications:

- Client Query module
- Price Update module
- Stock Analysis module

The first module handles queries from clients on their portfolios; the second module fetches prices from the stock exchange computer; and the third module runs price analyses on stocks for brokers. BOIS has decided to put the applications into a two-node MC/ServiceGuard cluster, with the modules running as three packages on two separate nodes. MC/ServiceGuard is used for two main reasons: to keep these applications available, and to give the information service the flexibility to run the application on a number of different servers at different times as the volume of usage changes and as they do maintenance.

The initial configuration of packages and data disks is shown in Figure 7.4. The Client Query package, running on Node 1, handles calls coming in from customers. Periodically, it refreshes its in-memory price list by obtaining current data from the Price Update module running on Node 2. The Stock Analysis module computes various allocation options for specific clients.

The Price Update module obtains new price data from the stock exchange at frequent intervals and provides this data to the Client Query and Stock Analysis modules when requested.

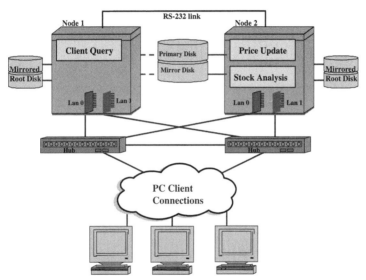

Figure 7.4 *HA Packages in a Brokerage Application*

Hardware Configuration

The following sections describe this example's configuration in detail. Note that many elements in the configuration could be modified for specific purposes. The goal, however, has been to provide HA by eliminating SPOFs.

Cluster Hardware

The cluster to be used by BOIS includes two HP 9000 L-Class systems. Two half-height slots per node are needed for the two Fast/Wide SCSI disk controllers to be used for disk storage. Two additional half-height slots per node will be used for Ethernet LAN connections.

Mirrored Disks

The cluster will be equipped with mirrored pairs of individual disks connected to the systems on different I/O channels. Each package requires its own set of disks for reading and writing. Figure 7.4 shows the kind of disk activation (access) needed by each package. Solid lines indicate exclusive access; dotted lines indicate that the disks are physically cabled to the node, but not being accessed by it. The Stock Analysis and Price Update packages are configured to obtain read-write access to separate sets of mirrored disks. Note that the Client Query module does not access any disk itself, since it obtains prices from the Price Update module over the LAN. Additional disks attached to the two channels may be used for other processing.

LAN Hardware and RS-232 Connections

An Ethernet configuration will be used, including two LAN interfaces per node attached to different hubs. Client requests for data come across redundant LAN segments from a separate group of systems on which user logons take place. Data and heartbeats will use one LAN interface, and an RS-232 connection between the two nodes will serve as a heartbeat backup in case of heavy user traffic on the LAN. The second LAN interface will serve as a standby.

Power

A total of two UPS units will provide protection in case of power loss. One UPS is used for Node 1 and the mirror disks for each package, and a second UPS is configured for Node 2 and the primary disks for each package. One SPU and one disk are connected to one power circuit; the second SPU and the other disk are connected to a different power circuit.

Responses to Failures

In the event of failures, what happens? If the Client Query package fails, it is configured to restart, and if the restart is successful, the client can reconnect immediately. If the node running the query software should go down, the Client Query package will be back on the other node in about a minute.

If the Price Update package fails, the Client Query package continues to operate, so clients will continue to obtain query results, but the data may be less fresh. The Price Update module will attempt to restart up to five times. If successful, the program will fetch a new price list at once, ensuring that prices will be refreshed within at least ten minutes, which the service guarantees to its clients. If the restart is not successful, the program will start up again on the other node within about a minute, and its first action will be to obtain a fresh update of stock prices.

If the Stock Analysis package fails, it will also attempt to restart before failing over to the other node.

If there is a disk failure, the MirrorDisk/UX software will continue writing data to the good disk until the other disk can be replaced.

In the event of SPU failure, the applications will continue running on the alternate node until the appropriate repair can be made on the failed node. After the loss of a node, of course, services will not be highly available until the repaired node re-enters the cluster. Figure 7.5 shows the state of the cluster after both the Price Update and Stock Analysis modules have failed over from Node 2 to Node 1.

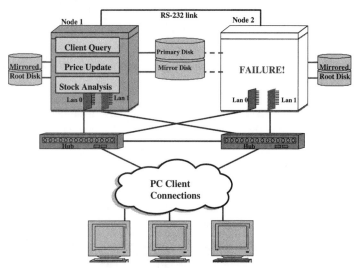

Figure 7.5 *Stock Applications After Failover*

Order Entry and Catalog Application

Pete's Clothiers is a mail-order and Internet-based seller of traditional menswear items. Customers can order through the mail, by telephone, or by Internet connections. Their home page is shown in Figure 7.6.

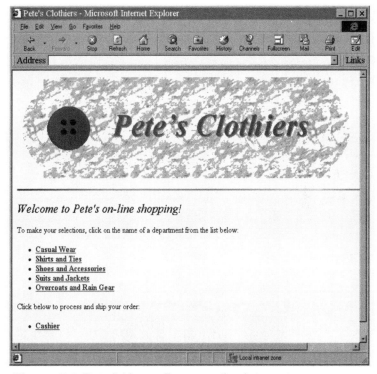

Figure 7.6 Retail Home Page on the Internet

Based in southern California, Pete's receives orders world-wide. The largest markets are the U.S., Canada and Mexico. Operations are ongoing 24 hours a day. There are slack periods, particularly from 12 midnight to 3 AM Pacific time. Some batch operations must be carried out, but there is still about an hour a day available for planned maintenance. The business has changed dramatically since 1996, when Pete's first went onto the Internet. This has required the IT department to provide better solutions for Web access to the company.

The High Availability Solution

The HA problem for Pete's boils down to the following: database systems must be available for order entry 24 hours a day, and the Web servers must also be highly available. Poor access time and periods of downtime mean lost orders and less customer satisfaction for Pete's Clothiers.

Order Entry Module

Pete's uses an on-line order entry system. Operators at the home office in San Diego handle phone orders that come in on an 800 number. Their workstations are connected by a LAN to Pete's HP 9000 servers.

Highly Available Internet Catalog Module

Pete's has put its entire catalog on-line and is allowing customers to enter their orders directly. This approach saves the expense of data entry operators, and gives customers access to the entire catalog on-line. It also provides a new approach to catalog publishing, with just-in-time information provided to customers without having to wait for the catalog in the mail.

The catalog is still mailed out, however, since the direct mail approach reaches more individuals than the Internet home page, which requires the effort of bringing up the catalog home page voluntarily. As the use of the Internet for business has increased, the availability of Pete's illustrated catalog on-line has become a competitive advantage that will be lost if the system is not available whenever customers wish to browse. Pete's expected a high volume of access to the Web server system, and decided to place the Internet home page and catalog database on separate servers. The volume is growing, however, and larger servers may be needed.

To ensure availability, the Information Resources department initially decided to create a ServiceGuard cluster running the order entry system as a package on one node, the Internet server as a package on a second node, and a third node serving as a standby node, which was also used for test and development. The nodes were connected by dual Ethernet subnets. The system used high-capacity disk arrays for mass storage. The database was an off-the-shelf relational database system; Pete's created customized applications for the client order entry stations.

Packages

One ServiceGuard package was created for the Web server, which was set up so that Internet-connected users could view the catalog files and process their own orders. A second package was used for the conventional phone-based order entry application, with operators entering customer orders on PC screens.

Orders were moved from the Web server system to the order entry system once a day by a batch program. Another batch job was used once a month to update catalog data and to modify prices, including specials. This job was designed to run when the catalog application was idle. During regular business hours, the packages were intended to run on separate nodes for performance reasons.

Original Hardware Configuration

A three-node ServiceGuard cluster solution was developed in 1996. The nodes were N-Class servers configured with dual Fast/Wide SCSI I/O controllers and two Ethernet LAN interfaces each, which were attached to Ethertwist hubs. Model 20 disk arrays were chosen for mass data storage, initially supporting up to 40GB of storage. The catalog initially was expected to use 40GB (when mirrored), and the orders database was expected to take up an additional 20 GB in the short term, with expansion expected. Either package was allowed to fail over to any other node. Performance would be affected by a failover, but not significantly during the slack periods, which were used for planned maintenance.

This configuration is shown in Figure 7.7. In normal operation of this cluster, one package runs on each of the two production nodes.

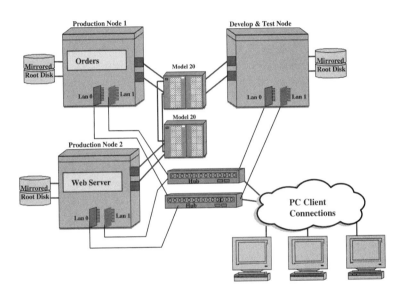

Figure 7.7 *Pete's Original Catalog and Order Entry Cluster*

Need for Expansion

By 1998, Pete's business had expanded to the point where the original configuration was no longer adequate. There was not enough bandwidth to handle the increasing volume of Web hits to the site, so a new strategy was needed. This included a group of dedicated Web server systems. In this case, HA for the Internet application was provided by replicating the servers without clustering. However, the main database was still protected with a ServiceGuard cluster. Cisco's Local Director was chosen to provide load balancing among the Web servers, and a FibreChannel-attached XP series disk array was installed to provide large storage capability, with room for further growth. This design is shown in Figure 7.8.

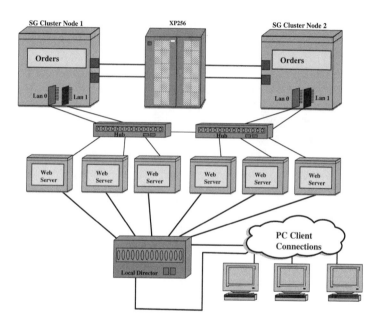

Figure 7.8 *Pete's Catalog System After Expansion in 1998*

Insurance Company Database

The Ever-Sure Company of Texas sells household and automobile insurance in 40 states. Ever-Sure wants to use a Service-Guard OPS Edition cluster running OPS software to consolidate all customer transactions in a single database while gaining the power of additional cluster hardware to keep transaction response time under two seconds. They have decided to partition their database according to insurance type, creating applications that access one cluster node for automobile insurance transactions and the other cluster node for household insurance transactions. An insurance agent in a local office connects to the database from a PC that is running a client application.

The Oracle database contains all the customer's personal data, as well as image data for vehicles and personal property that are being covered. The total size of data is currently 200GB. The plan is to use an HA disk array to provide mass storage as well as data redundancy through RAID 5.

Ever-Sure has been using separate Oracle databases on different servers, but wants to consolidate database administration by keeping all the data in a single database image, which can be backed up at one time and transferred to an off-site disaster recovery location. It is very important for Ever-Sure to be able to come on-line quickly following any disaster, so a replicated site is planned as well.

Two-Node OPS Configuration

A separate OPS instance runs on each node in a two-node cluster. Figure 7.9 shows the initial planned configuration.

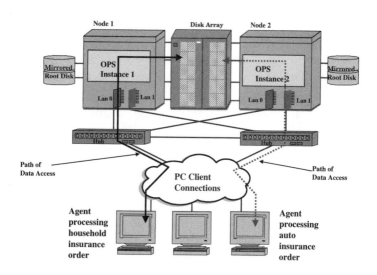

Figure 7.9 *ServiceGuard OPS Cluster for Ever-Sure*

In the figure, different paths of data access are shown for transactions involving customer records for different partitions of the database. An insurance agent processing a transaction in the area of household insurance accesses the OPS instance on Node 1. Another agent accesses the OPS instance on Node 2 because the transaction is for automobile insurance.

Responses to Failures

What happens if Node 1 leaves the cluster? In this event, all transactions are routed to Node 2, as shown in Figure 7.10. It is up to the client application to give the PC user a means to reconnect to Node 2 after a failure and re-route any transaction that was incomplete when the failure took place.

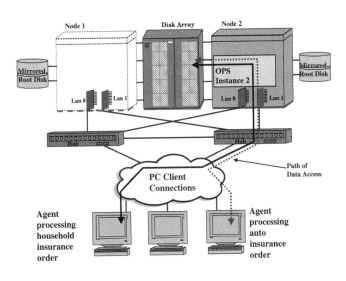

Figure 7.10 *Ever-Sure Cluster After Node Failure*

A node may leave the cluster because of failure (as indicated in the figure) or because the system administrator halts the node to perform maintenance.

Disaster-Tolerant Metropolitan Cluster for City Services

A populous southeastern U. S. coastal city decided in 1999 to develop a plan for protection of important city and county services in the event of a local disaster, including hurricane, major power outage, or fire. They decided to implement a metropolitan cluster for police and emergency dispatch systems, locating one data center on the coast, and the other data center about 20 miles inland. As part of this implementation, all police and emergency personnel would receive cellular phones and data appliances that could communicate via satellite with the servers over a data link regardless of where the servers were located.

In an emergency, dispatchers would report to the secondary data center and carry out their normal duties from the alternate location. Emergency personnel would be able to communicate with the servers via data links that switched their addresses to the secondary site. When the disaster was over, the database applications and data link addresses would fail back to the primary data center, and personnel would return to their usual offices.

A critical part of the design was the protection of the police and emergency records, but another aspect to be implemented was the use of the secondary data center for creating and archiving backups of all data. This would be done by taking BCs of the data volumes and archiving them to a tape library at the secondary site, which would be staffed for managing the backup operations and for restoring data when needed.

Hardware Configuration

The city decided to use MetroCluster with Continuous Access XP in a six-node cluster configuration that included two nodes at the primary data center and two at the remote data center, with two arbitrator nodes located at the recovery site. Storage would be on a pair of HP SureStore XP512 disk arrays, connected to each other via redundant ESCON links. The cables would be laid down in rights of way owned by the city and state. The backup solution at the secondary site was implemented using a DLT/48 tape library connected to both cluster nodes.

Figure 7.11 shows the basic configuration.

Software Packages

The packages running on the cluster include an emergency incidents module, a dispatcher's directory of personnel, a police blotter database, and modules that access regional and state databases for important police data. All these packages normally run on the primary site, Data Center A. Omniback software runs at Data Center B to provide backups of BCs created on the XP512 array at that site.

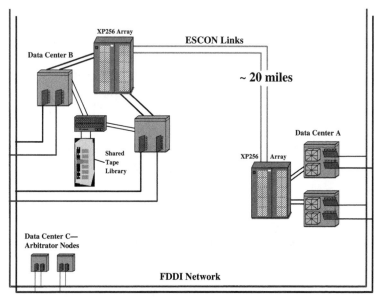

Figure 7.11 Metropolitan Cluster for City Services

Data Replication

Data replication between the two sites is done via the Continuous Access XP software, which coordinates the copying between the primary and backup sites. Continuous Access does two operations:

- Copies data to the backup site.
- Creates BCs on the backup site, which can then be used for backup operations.

262

Responses to Failures

If something happens to a node in Data Center A, packages can fail over to the other node within the local data center. So, in the event of a disaster, or when the cluster administrator wishes, packages from Data Center A can start up in Data Center B.

SAN Configuration for an Internet Service Provider

An ISP has decided to set up a service that allows clients to create files of various kinds and store and retrieve them as they would on their own computers. The user can create a document and store it, then access it from a different computer, or allow someone else to access it from a different location. Files supported in the system are of many types, but particular kinds include greeting cards, letters, memos, emails to friends, address lists, and financial records. All files are encrypted and stored in a form where users can obtain immediate access. Users are provided up to 100MB of storage free, and additional amounts carry a charge. In addition, the company derives revenue from advertising. The most significant challenges for the ISP are:

- To store the data efficiently.
- To provide quick access to files.
- To create and manage backups.
- To allow for expansion as the business grows.

Daily Operation

Customers connect through the Internet. A traffic managment system directs connections to one of a group of Web servers. The Web servers access the OPS database to validate access, then they allow customers to upload and download files or create different documents for storage and later retrieval. The ISP has decided to use a large OPS database to track customer data, together with a Web server farm for processing customer operations. A SAN configuration using several XP512 disk arrays provides for the actual storage of the OPS database as well as the customer files. Access to data is via high-speed switched Fibre-Channel connections that provide the fastest throughput.

Hardware Configuration

The configuration is shown in Figure 7.12. On the left is a two-node OPS cluster with N-Class servers. Each node is running an OPS instance that processes data about customers who are accessing the system. For example, customer billing data is stored in one set of database records, and pointers to customer files are stored in another.

Actual customer data is stored in the SAN, which is attached via FibreChannel switches to the nodes of the OPS cluster and to each Web server. When a customer requests access to a file, the OPS database provides its location in the SAN and passes this back to the Web server, which then allows the customer to upload or download their personal data.

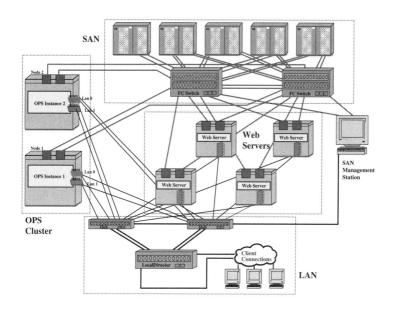

Figure 7.12 *ISP On-Line File Service with SAN*

SAN Management

The SAN is also cabled to a management workstation, which allows administrators to manage the data in the SAN. Two sets of tools are accessible from the workstation:

- SAN Manager LM, which allows LUN configuration within the SAN.
- Omniback, for managing backups, which account for a significant part of the overhead of the IT department.

An important characteristic of this configuration is its flexibility, because it allows the system to grow by adding more Web server systems, OPS cluster nodes, and disk arrays as the volume of business increases.

This configuration shows a number of different approaches to HA. The standard clustering technology is used to protect the customer database, whereas a Web server farm provides redundant Internet access to the company's services. Within the LAN, redundant Ethernet connections are provided, and within the SAN, there are redundant switched connections that provide HA as well as increased bandwidth. (Note that the diagram is incomplete; the managment operations are not fully included, and not all redundant connections are shown.)

CHAPTER 8
Glossary of High Availability Terminology

*T*his chapter contains a glossary of the terms used to describe HA concepts and the products that are used in creating HA solutions.

Adoptive Node

An alternate node to which MC/ServiceGuard could transfer control of a package. A package may have several adoptive nodes, though it has only one primary node.

Advanced Tape Services

These services allow you to attach tape libraries to more than one node in a ServiceGuard cluster to allow highly available backup operations and to permit efficient use of library facilities.

ADT

See *Average Downtime.*

AFR

See *Annualized Failure Rate.*

Alternate Node

See *Adoptive Node.*

Annualized Failure Rate

Annualized failure rate (AFR) is related to mean time between failures (MTBF) and mean time to repair (MTTR). It is calculated by dividing the sum of all failures in one hour, multiplying by 8760 hours to annualize the ratio, then multiplying by 100% to express the ratio as a percentage. Here is the formula for a 24x7x365 scheduled system:

$$AFR = \frac{1}{MTBF + MTTR} * 8760 * 100\%$$

As a predictive measure, the AFR gives an idea of the expected number of times a unit will fail in the period of a year. Thus, if the AFR is 200%, the unit would be expected to fail twice a year over the long term; if the AFR is 50%, the unit would be expected to fail once every two years, and so on.

Note, however, that since AFR is a function of both MTBF and MTTR, a low AFR may result from either a low MTTR or a high MTBF. Conversely, a high AFR may result from either a high MTTR or a low MTBF.

Architecture

See *HA Architecture*.

Availability

The percentage of time that a system is accessible to users over a period of time. Availability is determined by the following formula:

$$\% \text{ Availability} = \frac{\text{Elapsed Time - Sum (Inoperative Times)}}{\text{Elapsed Time}} * 100$$

Average Downtime

Average downtime (ADT) is a measure of the amount of time a unit is inoperative, that is, unavailable for use, per failure event. ADT is given by the following formula:

$$ADT = \frac{\text{Sum of Inoperative Times}}{\text{Total Number of Failures}}$$

Care must be used in defining what "inoperative" means. It is important to use this term consistently in defining the requirements for an HA system.

Campus Cluster

A type of cluster in which the nodes are isolated from each other in different buildings up to 10 km (6 miles) apart in such a way that an application can continue after the loss of a data center.

Cluster

A networked grouping of one or more SPUs and disk drives designed to support each other in the event of failure of one SPU or network component.

Cluster Lock

A device that provides a tie-breaker when a cluster splits into two equal-sized halves. May be implemented using either a *Lock Disk* or a *Quorum Server.*

ClusterView

A special tool that allows OpenView Network Node Manager (NNM) to manage cluster nodes for MC/LockManager and MC/ServiceGuard clusters. ClusterView can recognize cluster activities such as failover and re-formation.

Continental Cluster

A type of cluster architecture that allows applications to fail from a data center in one location to another location that is very distant. This architecture uses two ServiceGuard clusters and eliminates the cluster as a point of failure.

Continuous Access XP

Physical data replication services for the XP256 and XP512 disk arrays; used with metropolitan clusters and continental clusters.

Continuous Availability

Non-stop service. This term describes an ideal system state in which outages are completely masked to the user so that service never appears to be lost at all.

Custody

The current ownership of an MC/ServiceGuard package. Package custody is held by the node on which the package currently resides in a cluster.

Disaster-Tolerant

A type of cluster architecture that allows applications to continue following the loss of an entire data center. Metropolitan clusters and continental clusters have disaster-tolerant architectures.

Downtime

The duration of an outage in units of time such as hours or minutes. See also *Planned Downtime* and *Unplanned Downtime*.

EMC SRDF

A storage replication and duplication facility (SRDF) from EMC Symmetrix. A physical data replication facility used with metropolitan clusters and continental clusters.

EMS

See *Event Monitoring Service*.

Event Monitoring Service

A monitoring technology based on SNMP that lets you track system resources and either report problems to system administrators or take automatic action such as failing over a package.

Failure

Loss of a service. A failure is either a hardware or software problem.

Failover

The starting of a service on another computer following failure on the primary computer.

Fault Tolerance

The ability to mask system failures by switching to alternate components without the loss of connection or service. Fault tolerance is usually implemented through a highly redundant hardware system.

Grouped Net

Individual LAN segments connected to form a single redundant LAN subnet.

HA Architecture

The kind of cluster arrangement chosen to implement an HA solution. Examples are active/active, active/standby, and parallel database architectures. MC/ServiceGuard provides the functionality for the active/active and active/standby architectures; ServiceGuard OPS Edition provides the functionality for the parallel database architecture. See also *Disaster-Tolerant* and *Continental Cluster.*

Hardware Mirroring

The use of disk arrays to provide mirrored configurations. This is distinct from software mirroring, which is done through operating system (OS) tools such as Logical Volume Manager (LVM) and MirrorDisk/UX.

Heartbeat

TCP/IP messages that are sent between cluster nodes to ensure that all members of a cluster are running normally. When heartbeats are missed, a cluster re-forms, and if a node is lost, it will crash to prevent data corruption.

Highly Available

A broad term used to describe a computer system that has been designed to allow users to continue with specific applications even though there has been a hardware or software failure. Highly available systems protect applications from a failure of an SPU, disk, or network component.

Hot-Plug Capability

The ability of a computer system or peripheral such as a disk array to support the insertion of hardware components such as disks or cards while the system is powered up. Operator intervention at the keyboard may be needed to support hot-plug maintenance.

Hot-Swap Capability

The ability of a computer system to support the replacement of hardware components such as disks or cards without special preparation of the operating system or of the hardware itself.

LAN

A local area network (LAN) that is running network services. HA services depend on the LAN for communication of heartbeat messages and other information relating to the health of cluster components.

LAN Interface

The LAN interface card (LANIC) installed in a cluster node to support network services.

Lock Disk

A disk that is used to provide tie-breaking services to a cluster that is re-forming when equal groups of nodes are contending to start the cluster. Prevents *Split-Brain Syndrome*.

Logical Volume Manager

An HP-UX or Linux subsystem that creates a virtual disk from multiple segments of actual physical disks. One logical volume may consist of several disk drives that look like one logical drive to your data. See also *Shared Logical Volume Manager*.

Mean Time Between Failures

A metric used by hardware manufacturers to indicate the average time between component failures. Mean time between failures (MTBF) is given by the following formula:

$$MTBF = \frac{\text{Total Operating Time}}{\text{Total Number of Failures}}$$

Mean Time To Repair

An important measure of how a failure results in downtime. Mean time to repair (MTTR) is given by the following formula:

$$MTTR = \frac{\text{Sum of All Repair Times}}{\text{Total Number of Failures}}$$

It is important to understand how to define "repair time" in this formula. Is it the actual time to fix the problem, or does it include all the time from the failure itself to the time when service is restored? Does it include hardware only, hardware and software, or is it the whole system? One should be careful in comparing MTTR figures from different sources.

Metropolitan Cluster

A type of cluster architecture in which nodes can be separated from one another across a metropolitan area or in different cities that are within about 40-50 km (24-30 miles) of each other. This disaster-tolerant architecture provides protection against fire, flood, and localized power outage.

MirrorDisk/UX

A mirroring product that works with the HP-UX Logical Volume Manager (LVM) to provide software mirroring of disks for HA.

Mirroring

The practice of creating and maintaining more than one copy of data by writing to two or more disks instead of one.

MTBF

See *Mean Time Between Failures*.

MTTR

See *Mean Time To Repair*.

Network Node Manager

An OpenView application used for managing the individual systems in a large distributed network of computers. ClusterView, an extension to Network Node Manager (NNM), can be used to monitor HA clusters and nodes.

Node

One host system in an HA cluster, including its SPU and memory.

OpenView

An open systems framework provided by HP for monitoring and administering distributed computer systems. OpenView is a framework for several administration/monitoring tools, including:

- Network Node Manager (NNM)
- ClusterView
- Vantage Point
- Omniback

Package

A group of monitored services and resources that are configured to run together and that can fail over together to another node in a ServiceGuard cluster.

Planned Downtime

An expected outage whose duration is known in advance.

Primary Node

The first node on which a ServiceGuard package runs before there is a failover. The primary node and a list of potential adoptive nodes is coded in the package configuration file for each package.

Process Resource Manager

Process Resource Manager (also known as HP PRM) allows you to allocate CPU time to various process groups running on an HP-UX system. It can be used with MC/ServiceGuard or MC/LockManager configurations to adjust the priority of processes after a failover event or when packages move from node to node during maintenance operations.

Quorum Server

A software process running outside a cluster that is used to provide tie-breaking services to a cluster that is re-forming when equal groups of nodes are contending to start the cluster. Prevents *Split-Brain Syndrome.*

RAID

An acronym for redundant array of inexpensive disks. A RAID device consists of a group of disks that can be configured in many ways, including as a single unit or in various combinations of striped and mirrored configurations. The types of configurations available are called RAID levels:

- RAID 0: Disk striping

- RAID 1: Disk mirroring
- RAID 0/1: Sector-interleaved groups of mirrored disks. Also called RAID 1/0 or RAID 10
- RAID 2: Multiple check disks using Hamming code
- RAID 3: Byte-striped, single check disk using parity
- RAID 4: Block-striped, single check disk using parity
- RAID 5: Block-striped, data and parity spread over all disks

Redundancy

Duplication. Removing single points of failure (SPOFs) is usually accomplished by providing redundant software or hardware components for the parts that can fail.

Reliability

The inherent ability of a system to resist failure. This value is a probability. Reliability should be distinguished from availability, which can be measured on an actual system.

Relocatable IP Address

An IP address associated with an application package. This address can move from one computer system to another during failover so that users will always connect and reconnect to the same address.

Service

A process that is monitored by ServiceGuard. A service is normally an application program that is started by starting a package, and stopped by halting a package. If a service fails while the package is running, the package may be halted and restarted on an adoptive node.

Service Level Agreement

A document that spells out the expected periods of operation of an HA system together with acceptable intervals of planned and unplanned downtime. A service level agreement (SLA) may also specify the cost of providing computer services at a specific level and the penalties that apply for failure to provide the specified service.

ServiceGuard

A software product that allows you to customize and control your highly available system. With ServiceGuard, you can organize your applications into packages and designate the control of specific packages to be transferred to another SPU, or communications to be transferred to a standby LAN, in the event of a hardware failure on the package's original SPU or network.

ServiceGuard Manager

A graphical user interface (GUI) that provides maps and property sheets for cluster objects. ServiceGuard Manager displays the status of nodes, packages, and clusters with colored icons, and lets you store a snapshot of a cluster configuration in a file for later reference.

ServiceGuard OPS Edition

A software product that allows you to run Oracle Parallel Server (OPS) in a highly available cluster. ServiceGuard OPS Edition provides software coordination for the simultaneous access of shared disks by different nodes in the cluster.

Shared Logical Volume Manager

An OS subsystem that coordinates access to logical volumes by more than one computer system at a time, allowing concurrent access to data from different nodes within an HA cluster. The Shared Logical Volume Manager (SLVM) also allows disk resources to be switched quickly between the nodes of the cluster when a package moves from one node to another. See also *Logical Volume Manager*.

Shared Tape

See *Advanced Tape Services*.

Single Point Of Failure

Anything in a large computer system that results in the loss of service. When a failing element is not backed up by a redundant element, it is considered a single point of failure (SPOF).

SLVM

See *Shared Logical Volume Manager*.

Software Mirroring

The use of software to provide one or more extra copies of data written to disk. This is usually done through operating system (OS) software and extensions such as the Logical Volume Manager (LVM) and MirrorDisk/UX.

Split-Brain Syndrome

A condition in which two equal-sized subgroups of cluster nodes re-form a cluster independent of each other. This situation is prevented in ServiceGuard clusters by the use of the *Cluster Lock*.

SPOF

See *Single Point Of Failure*.

SPU

See *System Processor Unit*.

Subnet

Also called a subnetwork, this is a related group of IP addresses.

SwitchOver/UX

A cluster product that provides a standby processor to take over in the event of a primary processor failure. The standby reboots and restarts the application, after which users can restore their connections. The standby node assumes the identity of the primary node, including its IP address.

System Processor Unit

An individual computer in a highly available cluster system. It may have internal disks and backup power. Packages are assigned to individual system processor units (SPUs). Each SPU is considered to be a node in a ServiceGuard cluster. An SPU has one or more CPUs in it.

Transfer of Packages

When a cluster node or an associated network or service has failed, and the control of one or more packages is transferred to a functioning node.

Unplanned Downtime

An unexpected outage whose duration is unpredictable.

Vantage Point

A distributed system administration tool by HP that allows system administrators to manage distributed systems—including cluster nodes—from a central location.

Volume Group

In Logical Volume Manager (LVM), a volume group is a set of one or more physical disks that is managed by LVM as a single unit. Volume groups can be configured to be shared among cluster nodes, and logical volumes can be mirrored across channels to eliminate single points of failure (SPOFs).

Index

Numerics

5nines:5minutes 224
    architecture 226
    global control 231
    local control 229
    use of clusters 228

A

active/active
    cluster type 92
active/standby cluster 89
AdminCenter
    overview 155
adoptive node
    and ServiceGuard packages 96
Advanced Tape Services (ATS)
    features 211
agreement
    service level agreement 5

applications
    monitoring by ServiceGuard 98
    tailoring for cluster use 77
architectures
    5nines:5minutes 226
    active/active 92
    active/standby 89
    continental cluster 190
    disaster-tolerant 174
    metropolitan cluster 187
    parallel database 94
arrays
    disk arrays for data protection 49
automation
    use in high availability 30
availability
    continuous availability 6
    fault tolerance 6
    formula 14
    high availability cluster defined 79
    mean time between failures 17

fulfill your
needs

i n v e n t

Want to know about new products, services a
solutions from Hewlett-Packard Company — as
soon as they're invented?

Need information about new HP services to he
you implement new or existing products?

Looking for HP's newest solution to a specific
challenge in your business?

HP Computer News features the latest from HF

hpcomputer
news

4 easy ways to subscribe, and it's FREE:

- **fax** complete and fax the form below to
  (651) 430-3388, or

- **online** sign up online at
  www.hp.com/go/compnews, or

- **email** complete the information below ar
  send to hporders@earthlink.net, or

- **mail** complete and mail the form below t

  Twin Cities Fulfillment Center
  Hewlett-Packard Company
  P.O. Box 408
  Stillwater, MN 55082

reply now to receive the first year FREE!

name	title
company	dept./mail stop
address	

city	state	zip

email	signature	date

please indicate your industry below:

- [ ] accounting
- [ ] education
- [ ] financial services
- [ ] government
- [ ] healthcare/medical
- [ ] legal
- [ ] manufacturing
- [ ] publishing/printing
- [ ] online services
- [ ] real estate
- [ ] retail/wholesale distrib
- [ ] technical
- [ ] telecommunications
- [ ] transport and travel
- [ ] utilities
- [ ] other: _____

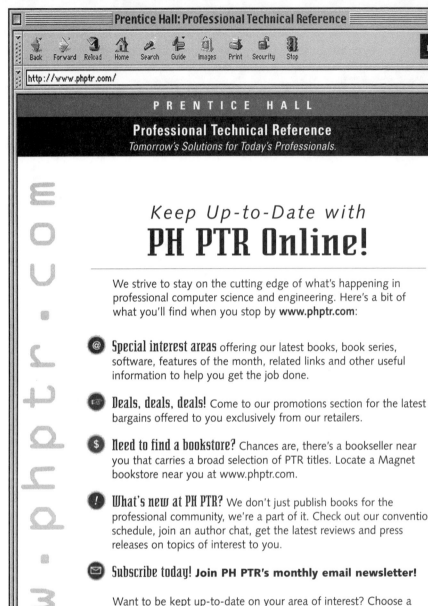